W9-DJK-094

Often Invisible

(Handouts
(a) Jones & Warberman summary
(b) CCWL document

Often Invisible

Counselling Gay & Lesbian Youth

Margaret S. Schneider
Ph.D., C. Psych.

Published by
Central Toronto Youth Services

WARNER MEMORIAL LIBRARY
EASTERN UNIVERSITY
ST. DAVIDS, PA 19087-3696

8/25/11

CENTRAL
TORONTO
YOUTH
SERVICES

27 Carlton Street, 3rd floor, Toronto, Ontario, M5B 1L2   977-1163
924-2100

© 1988, Central Toronto Youth Services

All rights reserved. No part of this book may be reproduced or transmitted in any form by any means without permission by the publisher, except for a reviewer who may quote brief passages in a review.

Cover Art: Sharon Beddard
Cover Design: Sharon Nelson
Typeset at On-Line Graphics, Toronto
Production by: Phoenix Productions Int'l, Toronto
Printed and bound by: Les Editions Marquis Ltée

HV 1449 .S34 1988
Schneider, Margaret S.,
 1950-
Often invisible

CANADIAN CATALOGUING IN PUBLICATION DATA

Schneider, Margaret, 1950-
   Often invisible: Counselling gay and lesbian youth

Bibliography; p. 135
Includes index.
ISBN 0-921708-00-9

1. Homosexuals - Counseling of.   2. Lesbians - Counseling of.
3. Youth - Counseling of.
I. Central Toronto Youth Services.   II. Title

HV1449.S34 1988   362.7'044   C88-094926-0

924 - 2100

Contents

PART II: COUNSELLING STRATEGIES AND ISSUES 71

Preface

Adolescent sexuality is a topic that most adults discuss with some discomfort. Whether the adolescents in question are their children, their clients, or their friends, the idea of sexually active teenagers raises many perplexing moral, emotional and practical issues for adults.

With few available resources about adolescent sexuality, without a vocabulary that is comfortable to use when discussing sex, and amidst a host of sexual taboos, adults are faced with the challenge of offering guidance to young people who are trying to learn about their own sexuality. When a discussion of adolescent sexuality turns to adolescent homosexuality, the challenge may seem insurmountable.

Social service providers in the Province of Ontario were directly confronted by the challenge of addressing the needs of lesbian and gay youth within the system, brought to the fore in the late 1970s by a number of major events.

One involved Tri-Aid, a charitable foundation, which applied for a license to open a group home in Toronto for gay street youth in 1975. The license was denied initially and at a subsequent appeal. However, experts testifying both for and against the licensing all agreed that gay and lesbian youth were not receiving the same quality of care that was available to their heterosexual counterparts.

Another event was the consolidation of all children's social services in 1977 under one Ministry, Community and Social Services (COMSOC), which caused some confusion among social service providers who were sometimes uncertain about where to seek assistance for their young clients. The Associate Deputy Minister at the time invited service providers to phone his office if they were unable to access appropriate services for their clients. He was inundated with calls. Many cases concerned lesbian or gay adolescents.

In response to the gap in services revealed by the two events, COMSOC explored ways to provide more effective service delivery to lesbian and gay youth who needed social service assistance. As a result, the Sexual Orientation and Youth Program was established in 1983, operating under the umbrella of Central Toronto Youth Services with two full-time staff members. In 1987 COMSOC committed core funding to the Program which is now a permanent part of Central Toronto Youth Services.

The Program is mandated to act as a resource for social service providers. To that end the following activities have been undertaken: (a) development and presentation of workshops, (b) development of written and audiovisual resource material, (c) collection of written resource material, (d) research, and, most recently, (e) case consultation.

This book was written to fulfill part of that Program's mandate. Its purpose is to provide helping professionals with a theoretical foundation, general information and analysis of clinical issues which are needed in order to work effectively with lesbian and gay youth, or with young people who are confused about their sexual orientation. The topics in the book reflect the range of questions and concerns which have been raised by participants in Program-sponsored workshops.

In the past five years of the Program's existence many people have contributed their time and energy to its continued development. The support of the past and present members of the Program's Advisory Group is gratefully acknowledged. The past and present members include: Brad Archer, Rosemary Barnes, Susan Bradley, Theresa Dobko, Eilert Frehrichs, David Kelley, Howard Marcovitch, Greg McClare, Kelly Rico, Mike Robinson, Heather Sproule, George Thomson, Anna Wellbourn, Mark Whitehead and Ken Zucker. Also gratefully acknowledged is the guidance and support of Terry Sullivan who was the Clinical Director at Central Toronto Youth Services. Bob Tremble, Coordinator of Training and Development of the Program made important contributions to several chapters of the book as did many members of Lesbian and Gay Youth Toronto. Thanks as well, to Margaret Schneider, Research Coordinator, who wrote the book. Of course, the Program would not have come into existence at all without the contribution made by Ontario's Ministry of Community and Social Services, including the staff of Central Region and the staff of the Toronto Area Office.

Grant Lowery
Executive Director
Central Toronto Youth Services

Forward

This publication marks one of a number of milestones for the Sexual Orientation and Youth Program at Central Toronto Youth Services. It also reflects a change in attitude which, although small and perhaps imperceptible to some, is quite striking to those of us involved since the inception of the Program. When the original committee assigned to examine the problems with services to gay and lesbian youth was formed in 1978, everything was done in secrecy; there were to be no discussions about the committee or its deliberations outside of a limited number of trusted associates. In official circles it was not acknowledged publicly that the committee even existed. The fact that there was a public conference in 1986 to mark the achievements of this project and that the Regional Director of Ontario's Ministry of Community and Social Services appeared there to support the Program signifies that the subject of gay and lesbian youth has begun to come out of the closet.

The initial impetus for the Program was the difficulty experienced by service providers during the late 1970s of attempting to find treatment resources for gay and lesbian adolescents. Most frontline workers knew little or nothing about homosexual adolescents and were generally uncomfortable in dealing with their needs. Thus the committee envisioned a staged process beginning with the development of resources and the education of frontline staff. It was expected that this phase would eventually lead to the development of residential resources for gay and lesbian youth. This initial phase of compiling the resources and educating the frontline workers has been undertaken by the Sexual Orientation and Youth Program.

Although it is obvious that attitudes towards homosexuality have begun to change, so have the needs changed. Perhaps the most noticeable changes have been the service needs related to AIDS:[1] providing information regarding safe sex and establishing guidelines for testing for example. The lack of a social support system for gay and lesbian youth continues to be a major problem. Less troublesome than previously, is the problem of finding residential placements for gay and lesbian adolescents, as it is for all adolescents.

The improvements which have occurred are to some degree due to the fact that frontline workers have been sensitized and educated to be more comfortable in dealing with gay and lesbian adolescents. However, without a visible, adequate social support system, accessible and open to all gay and lesbian youth, these young people will be vulnerable to all of the perils inherent in having to behave surreptitiously and to hide oneself in numerous ways.

If gay and lesbian youth can hope to look forward to an equal share in the joys and responsibilities of our society, it is essential to continue to sensitize service providers and the public, to equalize services, and improve support.

Although there are always issues, having watched the cooperative effort between government and Central Toronto Youth Services proceed so smoothly in such sensitive waters I feel optimistic that future collaboration will address many of the remaining issues.

Susan Bradley
Psychiatrist in Chief
Hospital for Sick Children
Toronto, Ontario

PART I

Understanding Homosexuality

We've always had gay adolescents though they were often invisible. They said nothing about it and neither did we. Then the kids started openly stating they were gay, and suddenly we didn't know how to respond.

Group Home Supervisor

In October, 1968, a police raid on a Greenwich Village gay bar sparked three days of rioting often referred to as the "Stonewall riots." This event was a watershed for the gay and lesbian population in North America. It marked the beginning of a movement which has fought for recognition and equality for gay men and lesbians, similar to the "Black is Beautiful" movement earlier in the decade. At the same time, psychological research was revealing the inaccuracy of stereotypes and myths about homosexuality. As a result, by the mid-1970s, gay men and lesbians had become increasingly willing to identify themselves openly. Many people were surprised to discover that among their friends, neighbors, colleagues, and family members there were lesbians and gay men.

Concomitantly, in the aftermath of the so-called sexual revolution, adolescents were becoming more aware of their own sexuality at an earlier age, and they were more willing to experiment and talk about their experiences. In the context of the new sexual freedom, homosexual adolescents who would have previously remained "closeted," began to identify themselves openly as homosexual. Consequently, social service providers were becoming aware that their caseloads included both gay and lesbian adolescents, and youngsters confused about their sexual orientation. Although these adolescents were not clients *because* they were gay or lesbian, workers felt compelled to respond in some way to their sexuality, but were unsure of the appropriate way to do so. Workers wanted to know whether their lesbian and gay clients should be encouraged to change their sexual orientation, and whether adolescents unsure of their sexual orientation should be encouraged to "go straight." They did not know what to do when male clients appeared wearing make-up or cross-dressed. Workers who were relatively comfortable when clients of the opposite sex were attracted to them were at a loss if a same-sex client was attracted to them. However, placement for gay or lesbian adolescents needing homes or residential treatment was the most difficult problem. Foster parents didn't want them, nor did group homes or institutions. Where would they live and sleep? With the same sex? With the opposite sex? By themselves? What if they made advances toward other youngsters? How would the other residents react? Frequently, behind these questions, lay a general feeling of discomfort with homosexuality.

These concerns, when viewed collectively, reflected a lack of familiarity, and, as a result, a lack of comfort with issues of sexuality in general, and homosexuality in particular. After all, few workers had much exposure to these areas either in their academic curriculum or in staff development in the workplace. In order to ensure that lesbian and gay youth received the same high quality services as other adolescents, workers would need a greater understanding of adolescent sexuality in general and more accurate information about homosexuality. They would also need to recognise how the counselling skills they already possessed could work as effectively with gay and lesbian clients. This book was developed as a response to the latter two requirements.

The remainder of this section is intended to lay the foundation for the rest of the book. It provides fundamental information and a theoretical framework which professionals need in order to work effectively with gay or lesbian youth. The topics covered include: a definition of homosexuality, causal theory, gender role and homosexuality, gay and lesbian relationships, gay and lesbian culture and community and the effects of stigmatization.

CHAPTER 1

Homosexuality Defined

Psychiatric, Moral and Ethical Issues

Homosexuality has been considered variously to be a crime, a sickness, and a sin. Myths and misleading stereotypes abound. A large part of the task in responding to the service needs of gay and lesbian youth is to distinguish these from reality.

As is still the case in some cultures, until the late 1800s, homosexual behavior was almost universally considered to be a sin and a crime. By the turn of the century, however, homosexuality came under the purview of the medical profession, as well as that of church and state, and was declared a mental illness (Katz, 1983). Indeed, research on homosexuality until the mid 1960s seemed to support this position.

The early research had two major methodological shortcomings (Gonsiorek, 1982; Gonsiorek, 1982a). The first was that the homosexuals studied were from a clinical population (i.e., individuals in psychotherapy). Frequently, comparison groups were not used; when they were, they consisted of non-clinical samples of heterosexuals. In consequence, and somewhat predictably, when clinical samples were compared to non-clinical samples, the homosexuals appeared to be more neurotic, unstable, and unhappy. The second flaw in the methodology was the lack of objective, quantitative data; subjective data, coming from psychiatrists' perceptions of their own cases were susceptible to biased interpretation. The lack of appropriate comparison groups (using random samples from the hetero-sexual and homosexual population) and the failure to collect objective data predisposed researchers to finding signs of mental disturbance in homosexuals.

In the late 1960s, research methods in the area became more rigorous. When homosexuals not in therapy were compared to heterosexuals not in therapy using objective, quantitative measures of personality, the two groups were found to be equivalent (Gonsiorek, 1982a). Although some mental health professionals remain unconvinced, on December 15, 1973 the American Psychiatric Association removed homosexuality *per se* from the roster of psychiatric disorders (Bayer, 1981). Only the category of Ego-dystonic Homosexuality remained in the *DSM-III* (American Psychiatric Association, 1983) and is included (under a different nomenclature — Sexual Disorder Not Otherwise Specified) in the *DSM-III-R* (American Psychiatric Association, 1987), the most recent edition. This will be discussed in Chapter 10.

Research conducted since the 1960s indicates that homosexuality is not a mental illness, that is, that homosexuality does not impair an individual's ability to lead a happy, productive life, nor does it interfere with the formation of friendships and intimate relationships; however, homosexuals can suffer from mental disturbance, just as heterosexuals can. Living in a society that generally rejects homosexuals is a source of stress for them and this can assault their self-esteem, generate internal conflict, and erode relationships. All of this is exacerbated when the individual is trying to remain closeted (Brooks, 1981).

The question, "Is homosexuality a moral illness?" cannot be answered by rigorous scientific investigation. However, theologians of all denominations are re-examining the translations, interpretations and context of the scriptures, with some reaching the conclusion that homosexuality is not a sin (Nelson, 1978). For example, the story of the destruction of Sodom and Gomorrah is often offered as proof of the sinfulness of homosexuality. However, some scholars contend that the sin of Sodom and Gomorrah was inhospitality to strangers, not homosexuality. The argument rests on the translation of the verb "to know," which can be taken literally or as a reference to sexual intercourse. The historical context of the story and the use of the verb in the Old Testament in general suggests that the sexual connotation is unlikely. In an article titled, "The Perennial Canaanites," Damien Martin (1984) examines this and other references to homosexual behavior in the Old and New Testaments. He suggests that the evidence for the sinfulness of homosexual behavior is not nearly as conclusive as we are often led to believe.

The context in which homosexual behavior exists has changed very much since Biblical times. Until very recently, homosexual behavior was equated with adultery, as was any sexual behavior outside the bonds of marriage. The concept of a loving, stable, monogamous relationship between persons of the same sex simply did not exist. Recent research indicates that homosexual relationships, like heterosexual relationships, can fulfill the emotional and familial needs of the partners. For some people, this new perspective on homosexual relationships alters the context of moral question. However, as Damien Martin (1984, pp. 356-357) points out, the overriding issue

> lies in the differentiation between personal belief and social policy. Whether a personal religious belief is held because of years of scholarly scriptural study, it is still personal. [People] have every right to believe that the Bible proves that homosexual acts are a sin but it is indefensible to claim that their interpretation of so ambiguous a text as the Bible justifies defining a code of conduct for others, especially one that is enforced by law.

While leaving this question of belief for the reader to decide, this material is written from the position that homosexuality is not a moral illness.

In many jurisdictions, homosexual acts are offenses under the law. The nature of the offence may include the following: (a) Sexual acts between two people of the same sex may be illegal; (b) The age of consent for homosexual acts may be higher than for heterosexual acts; (c) Homosexual acts may fall under the rubric of "indecent sexual acts" the definition of which is often vaguely worded and dependent upon "community standards" of decency; and (d) Particular sexual acts such as oral or anal sex (sodomy) may be illegal. Laws such as these are most often or exclusively applied to homosexuals, despite the fact that these acts are frequently practiced by heterosexuals. Similarly, laws pertaining to indecency may be used in discriminatory ways if community standards dictate that homosexual acts are *ipso facto* indecent. For example, while *The Joy of Sex* (Comfort, 1987) remains on bookstore shelves, the sale or distribution of the analogous homosexual version, *The Joy of Gay Sex* (Silverstein & White, 1977), has been prohibited from time-to-time. Laws regulating sexual activity vary from state to state in the United States (for example, as of 1982, sodomy is illegal in 25 of the 50 states [Peters, 1982]), but in Canada they are written into federal legislation. According to Canadian law, buggery and acts of gross indecency are indictable offences except when the persons involved are husband and wife or consenting adults over the age of 21. Challenges to these laws have been on the grounds that (a) the state has no business in the bedrooms of the nation, and (b) the laws are unconstitutional because they are applied discriminately against homosexuals. These challenges have been largely unsuccessful, making homosexuals vulnerable to prosecution.

A Psychological Definition of Homosexuality

Homosexuality can be defined using precisely the same terms employed to define heterosexuality. Heterosexuality is emotional and physical attraction to persons of the opposite sex, and perhaps more importantly, it includes falling in love, caring for, and making a commitment to a person of the opposite sex.

Similarly, homosexuality entails emotional and physical attraction to persons of the same sex — the most salient difference being that the partner is of the *same* sex. Yet, the tendency is to focus exclusively on the sexual aspect of homosexuality. In fact, many of the myths about homosexuals revolve around sexual behavior such as, "homosexuals are excessively interested in sex" or "homosexuals are interested in seducing heterosexuals and children."[3] It is important to question the source of this misplaced focus on sexuality.

Often the descriptor "homosexual" is allowed to obscure everything else about a person. After all, it is an unusual characteristic, all the more mysterious because of the mythology and stigma attached to it. Furthermore, unlike heterosexuals, homosexuals sometimes need to openly and overtly identify themselves as lesbian or gay (see Chapter 11). For this reason they become labeled for their sexuality, unlike most heterosexuals. As a consequence of the inordinate focus on that single characteristic, many people tend to think of it as if it were spelled, homoSEXuality.

If you think of people that you know who are "straight," it is probable that you think of them as skiers, neighbors, gardeners, or lawyers. It is unlikely that you think of *them* as first and foremost, *hetero*SEXuals. When you think of people who are gay, is it their sexual orientation which looms as their most important feature? If it does, the challenge is to place each individual's sexual orientation in perspective as only one of a wide range of traits characteristic of each individual.

In summary, homosexuality differs from heterosexuality only in that the object of attraction is a person of the same sex. Within both, there is a wide range of behaviors, sexual and otherwise. Thus, homosexuality (like heterosexuality, or bisexuality) is one of several possible pathways in the development of one's sexuality.

Who are Homosexuals?: A Look at the Statistics

In the late 1940s, Alfred Kinsey and his associates conducted a massive study of sexual behavior in the United States (1948, 1953). One of the most remarkable findings was the wide variability in sexual experiences. Relatively few people were found to be exclusively heterosexual or homosexual. Many heterosexuals reported having some same-sex sexual experiences, often during adolescence, and/or homosexual feelings or fantasies. Consequently, Kinsey depicted sexual orientation as a continuum on a seven-point scale. At one extreme were the exclusively heterosexual and at the other were the exclusively homosexual; gradations of experiences were in between. In the middle were those whose heterosexual and homosexual experiences were more or less equally balanced.[4]

According to Kinsey's study (and comparable ones in Europe), about five per cent of the adult female population and about 10% of the adult male population is homosexual (Marmor, 1980). These may be conservative figures, since they were calculated at a time when the homosexual population was even more hidden than at present. The actual proportions might be higher (although less frequently cited researchers estimate the figure to be closer to four percent [Bullough, 1981; Hunt, 1974]). In addition, about 10% of the population is bisexual,[5] falling in the middle of the Kinsey scale while 15 to 20% had had some homosexual feelings or experience, but identified themselves as heterosexual. To summarize Kinsey's complex findings, nearly 40% of the population is either homosexual, bisexual, or has experienced some same-sex sexual contact or feeling at some time in their lives. Consequently the precise definition of who is a homosexual is a controversial issue in itself (Paul & Weinrich, 1982).

The relevance of these figures lies in what they reveal about the world in which we work and live. Those who live in large cities can reasonably assume that some of their neighbors, colleagues, even friends, are gay or lesbian. Teachers can estimate that about five to ten per cent of the young people in their school will grow up to be gay or lesbian. That means 25 to 50 students in a school of 500 will define themselves as gay or lesbian when adult. Social service providers can make the same inference about their client load.

These statistics may seem high to service providers unaware of who their gay and lesbian clients are. It is often assumed that homosexuals are easily identified by their mannerisms, speech, and gender-role behavior. This is, in fact, a myth. It is not necessarily easy to identify these young people, since the majority of lesbians and gay men are indistinguishable from heterosexuals (Berger, Hank, Rauzi, & Simkins, 1987; Marmor, 1980). (See Chapter 2.)

In addition to the gay and lesbian youngsters, a significant proportion of young heterosexuals have had some homosexual feelings or engaged in some homosexual behavior during adolescence; they may be disturbed or confused by their experiences (see Chapter 10). In summary, the statistics suggest that the issue of sexual orientation may be a concern to a substantial number of adolescents, whether heterosexual, homosexual or uncertain of their sexual orientation.

Causes of Homosexuality

What causes homosexuality is a question frequently asked by workers, parents of lesbian and gay children and the adolescents themselves. Theories cite both environmental and biological factors. The most common environmental theories include (a) Freud's theory (1905) that all individuals go through a homosexual developmental phase and can be fixated there due to certain kinds of life experiences; and (b) the belief that homosexuality in males is the result of a domineering mother and a cold, distant father. Neither of these theories has been substantiated with scientific evidence. In fact, a study by Bell, Weinberg and Hammersmith (1981) indicated no differences in the family backgrounds of heterosexuals and homosexuals.

There is also no evidence that sexual abuse causes homosexuality. There are lesbians and gays who have been abused sexually, just as there are heterosexuals who have been abused sexually. Abuse does not affect sexual orientation, although it may create confusion (see Chapter 11).

Research into the possible biological causes of homosexuality have shown that genetic programing does not influence sexual orientation directly; that is, there is no gene which determines sexual orientation (Money, 1980). However, researchers have investigated the relationship between hormones and homosexuality. Hypothesizing that gay men had lower levels of androgens (male hormones) than heterosexuals, researchers compared hormonal levels with contradictory results. Most studies showed no differences in levels of androgens. Some showed that homosexuals had lower levels than heterosexuals while others showed that homosexuals have higher levels (Sanders, Bain, & Langevin, 1985).

Other researchers have investigated the prenatal influence of hormone levels on sexual orientation. For example, Dörner (1976, 1977 cited in Tourney, 1980) has found that rats and hamsters experiencing a temporary prenatal deficiency in androgens were homosexually aroused as adults. The extent to which these types of studies are relevant to the human experience of sexuality, however, is open to debate.

There has been no theory to date backed by scientific research which adequately explains the origins of an individual's sexual orientation, homosexual or heterosexual. When lesbians and gays describe how they became aware of their sexual orientation a variety of patterns emerge (see Chapter 6). This suggests that the causes may be different for different people.

A focus on causes of homosexuality has some important implications. Causes are usually sought for things which are negative or pathological such as war, cancer or schizophrenia. The underlying assumption is that if cause could be determined then a cure could be found. To ask about cause implies that it would be preferable to cure or prevent homosexuality if possible. Certainly some people take this position. However, since research has supported the belief that homosexual relations are viable and legitimate, a search for cure or prevention is irrelevant. A less biased and less value-ladened focus (and perhaps a more interesting one) would be to examine the causes of sexual orientation and sexual expression in general.

When lesbian or gay clients or their parents ask what causes homosexuality there is often an unspoken, underlying question. Clients may really want to know if they can be "cured" or if their parents are to blame. Parents of lesbian and gay children may be asking similar questions: "Is it my fault?" "Can she be cured?" The worker will need to address the possible underlying messages when the question of cause is raised.

CHAPTER 2

Gender Role, Identity, and Homosexuality

It is a common misconception that gay men are effeminate and lesbians are masculine. In a survey of social service providers conducted by the Sexual Orientation and Youth Program (Schneider & Tremble, 1985), one third of about 300 respondents believed in these stereotypes. Evaluating the accuracy of these stereotypes requires an examination of the personal and cultural meanings of masculinity and femininity in society today, the origin of the stereotype and its social context, and the significance of cross-gender behavior.

The concept of gender role is distinct from sex, that is, the biological status of being either male or female. It is also distinct from sexual identity, which is an individual's psychological identity as male or female. For example, both heterosexual and homosexual men have a male sexual identity. They feel like males, and are satisfied being males. Similarly, heterosexual women and lesbians have a female sexual identity. They feel like females and are satisfied being females. This is in contrast to transsexuals whose sexual identity is in conflict with their biological status. For example, a biological male transsexual feels, psychologically, like a female. He would describe himself as a female trapped inside a male body. He behaves like a female and may be a candidate for a sexual reassignment, that is, a sex-change operation. Similarly, a biological female transsexual feels, psychologically, like a male. Transsexuality is not the same as homosexuality.

Gender role refers to all the traits, behaviors, and attributes which are socially defined as either masculine or feminine. These traits, however, are not fixed and vary cross-culturally at any given time. In North America, for example, women are considered to be emotional and irrational; while in Iran, they are seen as cold and logical. North American women are said to be gossips, yet in parts of the Philippines it is men who allegedly cannot keep a secret (Tavris & Offir, 1977). Gender roles also vary within a culture as time passes. Over the past two decades, North Americans have seen a tremendous change in what are considered to be appropriate professions for men and women. Female doctors, lawyers, and engineers are no longer the exception, while more men are becoming involved in fields such as child care. These examples illustrate how notions of masculinity and femininity are socially defined and subject to change, although, at any given time, a consensus exists about what constitutes stereotypically masculine or feminine behavior. Very few of us, male or female, adhere totally to either stereotype. Most of us possess both masculine and feminine traits to a greater or lesser extent.

The stereotypes of the effeminate gay male and the super-masculine lesbian are extreme caricatures of contemporary notions of masculinity and femininity. The stereotypical image of the effeminate gay man does not truly resemble even the most traditional of women; likewise the stereotypical image of the "butch" lesbian is not very much like the image of most heterosexual men. Workers may occasionally encounter a lesbian or gay male who does behave or dress in a stereotypical way. However, cross-gender behavior and appearance is not inherent to homosexuality and no generalizations about stereotypical gay and lesbian youth can be made in this regard.[6]

Origins of the Stereotypes

Until the late 1800s, homosexuality in Western cultures was considered to be merely deviant sexual behavior, condemned by the church and punished by the state. By 1880, however, the medical profession was recognizing the psychological component accompanying homosexual behavior — that it could also involve emotional attachment. For the first time the profession began to make a distinction between heterosexuality and homosexuality and the concept of sexual orientation was born. It is important to remember that this was taking place in a Victorian era in which biology was destiny.

> The concept of true woman and true man equated biological female-ness and maleness with those constellations of qualities collectively called "femininity" and "masculinity." No basic distinction was made

... between biological sex and culturally constructed womanhood and manhood. (Katz, 1983, p. 139)

In this social context, homosexuals (sometimes referred to as "inverts") were perceived to be, and perceived themselves to be, people who wished to be the opposite sex, because they had feelings (i.e. attraction to their own sex) which were "proper and exclusive" to the opposite sex.

> Feeling determined being... If a male felt the alleged emotions of a female, he must be a female or, at least, a "mental Hermaphrodite." The belief or claim that one was "really" the other sex was a way for one to justify to others and to oneself, within the premises of the time, erotic attraction to the "same" sex. (Katz, 1983, p. 145)

Thus, the image of the gender-atypical homosexual was born. A classic example of this can be found in Radclyffe Hall's *The Well of Loneliness*, (1976) the tragic story of a lesbian who dressed and behaved like a man.

At a time when polarized gender roles existed for heterosexual men and women, homosexuals were attempting to make sense of apparently non-sensical feelings and to find some normalcy in relationships. They found consistency between their feelings and their sexual identity by adopting one or the other of the polarized gender roles which they saw among heterosexuals. The only model for homosexual couples was the heterosexual man and woman with their clearly defined gender roles. With no other model, homosexual couples adopted the prevailing roles with one person affecting the role of the stereotypical male while the other adopted that of the stereotypical female.

A tremendous social pressure existed in male and female homosexual circles alike to be either "butch" or "femme" and those who would not conform were shunned. (There was, by the mid-1950s a dearth of femme lesbians as everyone wanted to be butch [Lynch, 1985]. It was, after all, the butch, like the heterosexual male, who held the power and prestige.) As gender roles in society at large began to change, becoming more flexible, gender atypical behavior among homosexuals began to disappear. Today young gays and lesbians are far less likely to behave stereotypically (Schneider, in press), and role-playing in couples has virtually disappeared (Cardell, Finn, & Marecek, 1981; Hedblom & Hartman, 1980; Lynch & Reilly, 1985; Schneider, 1986).[7]

Research on Gender Role and Sexual Orientation

The correlation between gender role and sexual orientation is a compelling question for researchers. Several retrospective studies, investigating the childhood experiences of adult gays and lesbians have indicated that gay males are more likely to have engaged in "feminine" behavior as children than heterosexual males. That is, they preferred girls' games and toys, avoided rough and tumble play, preferred female peers, and were regarded as sissies (Bell, Weinberg, & Hammersmith, 1981; Bieber, 1962; Saghir & Robbins, 1973; Whitam, 1977). Lesbians were more likely than heterosexual women to have been tomboys as they were growing up (Saghir & Robbins, 1973; Whitam, 1977). However, these results must be interpreted with caution, because of the following methodological problems.

One weakness with the research is that these and other similar studies have enlisted research participants from clinical populations or through notices in gay bars or gay publications. This affects any generalization because there is reason to believe that gender-atypical behavior may be more frequent among these groups. Research has indicated that homosexuals who have been in therapy are more likely to report childhood gender-atypical behavior (Bell, et al, 1981). Furthermore, since gender-atypical male homosexuals tend to have lower self-esteem than those who are not, they may be more likely to be found in a clinical population. There is also reason to believe that gender-atypical behavior may be more frequent among those who are openly gay enough to frequent known gay venues.

Another problem is that all these studies are retrospective and recall of childhood events may be unreliable. Homosexuals may be more likely than heterosexuals to recall and report childhood gender atypical behavior for two reasons. Firstly, it may be more acceptable for them to do so. Secondly, they may be more likely to remember such behavior, because, it might in retrospect, be perceived by them as a significant milestone in the coming-out process.

The final problem is that most of the research concerns gay men, not lesbians, and generalizing from the male to the female experience would not be justifiable.

Even if the research methods were impeccable, generalizing about the connection between gender role and homosexuality would be difficult. Not all homosexuals recall cross-gender behavior as they were growing up, while some tomboys and sissies grow up to be heterosexual.[8] In fact it is impossible to predict whether a particular effeminate boy will grow up to be homosexual, heterosexual, or transsexual (Green, 1980). Furthermore, research on gay and lesbian adults indicates that few gay men are effeminate in personality, dress, manner, preferred activities or occupations and lesbians are not usually masculine (Bell & Weinberg, 1978; Berger, et al, 1987; Delora & Warren, 1977; Gagnon & Simon, 1973; Storms, 1980; Warren, 1974). For example, in the Bell and Weinberg study of hundreds of gay men, the occupations of gay men and straight men were remarkably similar. In Storms' study, gays and lesbians were indistinguishable from heterosexuals on personality measures of masculinity and femininity.

Some research, as well as anecdotal evidence, suggests that gender-atypical behavior in lesbians and gay men can be culturally induced. One recent study indicates that the degree of femininity in homosexual men is directly related to the degree of gender-role stereotyping and anti-homosexual feelings in the culture (Ross, 1983). Stereotypical behavior may be a reaction to, or an outgrowth of, rigid gender roles and societal intolerance of homosexuality in general. The stereotype and its relevance is changing for the generation of gay men and lesbians born during and after the baby boom. Recent research involving lesbians between ages 18 and 22 indicates that the "butch" lesbian is, in their eyes, an image from the past (Schneider, in press). As mentioned earlier, contemporary gay and lesbian couples are unlikely to adopt masculine or feminine roles. The image of the typical gay male has changed over the last decade as well from effeminate to preppy and athletic. These changes evolved concomitantly with an increased tolerance of homosexuals in North America and the increased flexibility of gender roles in society at large. In fact, the popular youth culture cultivates an androgynous look. If, as this evidence indicates, the relevance and nature of stereotypical cross-gender behavior among homosexuals can be mediated by cultural context, then cross-gender behavior must be, at least in part, a function of cultural context, rather than an inherent part of homosexuality.[9]

In summary, although research points to some connection between gender role and homosexuality, the nature of that connection is unclear, and it would still be unwise to make generalizations.[10] However, there are two major implications. Since discomfort with gender-role deviance is one source of homophobia (see Chapter 5), understanding that cross-gender behavior is not an intrinsic part of homosexuality can contribute to greater tolerance (although one may want to examine why gender-role deviance is disconcerting). In practical terms, social service providers should be loath to form judgments about their clients' sexuality based on the presence or absence of gender deviant behavior, and when confronted with such behavior may want to question its significance.

CHAPTER 3

Lifestyle, Community and Culture

Homosexuality has been referred to as an "alternate lifestyle," as if the lives of homosexuals are essentially different from those of heterosexuals. In this chapter, and in a later examination of lesbian and gay relationships (Chapter 4), it will become apparent that the so-called gay lifestyle is nonexistent. There do exist, however, identifiable lesbian and gay communities and cultures which will be described in this chapter. It will be useful to keep in mind for the purposes of this examination of lifestyle, community and culture among lesbians and gays, the following definitions from the Webster's New Collegiate Dictionary (1982):

Lifestyle: An individual's typical way of life.

Community: A body of persons having a common history or common political, social, or economic interests: A group of people with a common characteristic or interest living together within a larger society.

Culture: The customary beliefs, social forms, or material traits of a racial, religious, or social group.

Lifestyle

The film, "Michael, a Gay Son" (Glauson, 1980) is a fictional dramatization of one family's struggle to accept the homosexuality of one of its members. One scene shows the fictional family in therapy, discussing their feelings about Michael's disclosure that he is gay. In the course of the discussion, Michael's father expresses how upset he is with "Michael's lifestyle" although he does not explain what that means to him. If he had been asked to do so, he might have expressed the belief that there is a "gay lifestyle" — a unified way of life, probably characterized by unbridled promiscuity and gender-atypical behavior. Michael's father might have been relieved to know that there is no single "gay lifestyle," just as there is no single "straight lifestyle." Belonging to a stigmatized minority because of attraction to the same sex is the only factor unifying gay men and lesbians. Gays and lesbians have a full range of lifestyle options open to them. Choices about the quality of intimate relationships, friendships and other social interactions are not limited by one's sexual orientation.

Culture

Although the "gay lifestyle" is non-existent, there are gay and lesbian communities and identifiable gay and lesbian cultures which are relevant to the lives of homosexuals to varying degrees. Gay and lesbian cultures have evolved out of the stigmatization which sets gay men and lesbians apart. It is the need for an historical context, for an artistic medium through which to express hopes, dreams, aspirations and sorrows and for an artistic tradition which portrays gay and lesbian lives and relationships with integrity and credibility, which forms the foundation for gay and lesbian culture. Lesbian culture is distinct from gay culture in so far as it has, in addition to an artistic tradition, a foundation of social and political theory fostered by connections with the feminist movement.

Neither gay nor lesbian culture is only for gays and lesbians. The works of Rita Mae Brown, Jane Rule, Scott Symonds and Harvey Fierstein, for example, have attracted a large general audience. While serving a special function for lesbians and gays — i.e. legitimization and affirmation — artistic works from the gay and lesbian cultures have appeal because they reflect human experience from a particular perspective, as do works arising from Jewish, black, French Canadian or Native Canadian cultures.

Community

Gay and lesbian communities emerged in response to stigmatization just as the cultures did. Whether they are large, visible urban communities, or dispersed friendship networks in rural areas, gay and lesbian communities serve a number of essential functions. First, they provide a safe place for lesbians and gays to socialize, without fear of attracting attention or reprisals from queer-bashers. (A same-sex couple who wants to go dancing is ill-advised to do so at the local heterosexual club.)

Second, community activities provide a casual, informal opportunity to meet new lesbian or gay friends and to share common experiences and benefit from mutual support. This function of the community is frequently misunderstood. Heterosexuals are often puzzled by the need for gay baseball leagues or lesbian soccer leagues. To understand this need, it is important to recognise an important function of recreation. Beyond the value and pleasure of the activity itself, recreation provides a setting for talking with friends about issues of mutual concern. Thus recreation in a lesbian or gay setting is an opportunity to discuss concerns common to gays and lesbians (for example, how to deal with homophobia in the work place, or coming out to parents) in a relaxed and informal atmosphere. Contrary to what some think, it does not ghettoize lesbians and gays. After all, gays and lesbians work in the larger community, most live outside the confines of an identifiable gay and lesbian neighborhood, and most socialize with both heterosexual and homosexual friends.

As will be discussed in Chapter 6, contact with other gays and lesbians is an integral part of the coming-out process in that it promotes the development of self-esteem as a gay or lesbian individual. The community is not the only place to meet lesbian and gay peers, and, indeed, gays and lesbians do not always maintain their initial contact with the community once they establish their own friendship networks. However, for most people, the gay and lesbian community is the springboard for establishing a network of lesbian and gay friends.

Because of media attention, bars and steambaths are what many people think of when they think of gay and lesbian communities. Unfortunately, these are one of the most visible components of gay and lesbian communities, and they have become a ubiquitous part of the mythology of gay sexual excess. Of course, bars and steambaths do exist. (It is important to note that steambaths and other venues for casual, anonymous sex are exclusively a gay male phenomena.) However, defining gay and lesbian communities in these limited terms is analogous to representing heterosexual communities in terms of tenderloin, macho bars and swinging singles clubs. Obviously, neither are adequate representations of either community.

In large metropolitan areas, gay and lesbian communities may be visible because activities take place in a particular geographic area. Most are identified openly as gay or lesbian and are advertised in gay or lesbian publications. Activities include organized sports leagues, outdoor clubs, counselling services, political groups, religious groups, potluck suppers and peer support facilities. In addition to this visible community there are a variety of friendship networks which, although invisible, can nonetheless be loosely called communities. Thus, to refer to the gay and lesbian population as a single community is to oversimplify.

In small towns and rural areas the gay and lesbian community may consist of geographically dispersed friendship networks in which people gather together for social events in private homes. Regardless of the structure, the functions of these communities are the same.

Adolescents in the Gay and Lesbian Community

For gay and lesbian adolescents, contact with a community is a milestone in the coming-out process. It is often the first opportunity to get to know other homosexuals and to find friends and/or role models. Through this contact they come to appreciate the diversity of the gay and lesbian population, and observe first hand that homosexuals can be happy, productive individuals. These observations are essential in developing a gay-positive outlook, and for that reason, access to a community is essential to the well-being of gay and lesbian adolescents.

Most gay men and lesbians remain isolated until after adolescence, especially those who live outside of large cities. Those young people who do manage to find a lesbian and gay community do so using a variety of strategies. They meet gay or lesbian peers by chance at school or at work. They search the phone book for the words "gay," "lesbian," or "homosexual." They go downtown searching for the community they have been told is there and fortuitously find a publication, bookstore, flyer, or bar. Some young men start frequenting the areas of the city known to be homosexual cruising areas, hoping to be picked up.

Adolescents in rural areas are less likely to have access to the friendship network in their area since it is neither visible nor localized in the way that communities in the cities are. Consequently, rural youth are more likely to be isolated until they are old enough to move to a city or lonely enough to run away. (See Moses and Bruckner [1982] and Belitsos [1983] for discussions of special problems for rural lesbians and gays.)

Unfortunately, there are few niches for youths in gay and lesbian communities. Activities are largely adult organized and adult focussed, and adolescents are prohibited by law from entering bars. Those who can pass for the legal drinking age consider themselves lucky to gain access to the bars — the most visible setting for meeting friends, socializing and dancing. Yet, in doing so they do not necessarily gain access to the adult world. Adult homosexuals are often reluctant to associate with adolescents, primarily because they fear accusations of recruiting or seducing minors —a charge to which they are particulary vulnerable. What is self-preservation for adults often seems to youth like rejection and ageism.

Young people themselves are ambivalent about the bar scene. They recognize that the alcohol-focussed, sexually loaded environment is not appropriate for young people and sometimes find it difficult to cope with. Yet they continue to frequent the bars, which after all, are places to dance, meet friends, and provide a springboard to the rest of the community.

There are alternatives to the bar scene. To varying degrees, these alternatives are open to young gay males and lesbians, but they are largely populated by adults and, as such, hold little interest for teenagers. While socializing between teenagers and adults can be rewarding for both groups, it leaves much to be desired as the sole option for adolescents. It also presents some conflicts: after a baseball game, if the team goes out for a beer is the underage adolescent permitted to join in?

The social needs of gay and lesbian adolescents are the needs of all youth. In the words of a young lesbian, "I want somewhere to be normal and lesbian. I would like to do regular, normal things with other lesbians." They want to go on trips, go dancing, go camping, or simply hang out in casual surroundings. Sometimes they need to do these things in a gay or lesbian environment. These opportunities for youth are not readily available in the gay and lesbian community. Until they are, social service providers will have to be creative in assisting lonely or isolated lesbian or gay adolescents.

Using Community Resources

The lesbian and gay community is a valuable resource for workers. Some of the services in the community may provide helpful educational material. For example, a group called Parents and Friends of Lesbians and Gays, which has chapters in many large cities, distributes a booklet answering the most common questions asked by parents of lesbian and gay children. Becoming familiar with lesbian and gay cultures and the local community helps workers appreciate the context in which their clients will socialize and learn about the meaning of being gay or lesbian.

By analogy, a Caucasian worker with a Caribbean or Asian client (or vice versa) needs to know something about the client's cultural background and local community. The worker can utilize community resources to learn more about the client's perspective and may want to find out about resources in the community which may be useful for the client. Similarly, when a client is lesbian or gay, knowledge of the community and culture are essential if the worker is to appreciate the implications when clients discuss local venues, groups and activities. Furthermore, if young lesbian and gay clients need the worker's help in initiating contact with lesbian and gay peers, workers will need to know what the possibilities are.

Naturally, workers will reject bars as appropriate vehicles, just as they would for young heterosexual clients seeking social outlets. If there is no local youth group, workers may rely upon personal contacts with gay or lesbian professionals in seeking out peer support, or may decide to initiate a peer support group for young homosexuals within the social services agency. Failing these options, workers and clients may be stymied. The best workers may have to offer the client is support in tolerating the isolation until the client is old enough to participate in adult-focussed activities.

Regardless of whether or not a community is accessible, the role of workers is to foster the understanding that lifestyle choices are not restricted. The options for socializing for gays and lesbians are as varied as they are for heterosexuals, and in exercising their options, young people must not feel bound by the myths and stereotypes about the so-called "gay lifestyle".

CHAPTER 4

Is What They Say About Gay and Lesbian Relationships True?

Young people are given many expectations of their future lives and inti-mate relationships. They anticipate dating, falling in love, and eventually establishing a long-term partnership, usually involving marriage and children Their adolescent experiences underscore these expectations. Many activities take place in a boy-meets-girl context and intrinsic to most films, music, and advertising is the heterosexual relationship. Although changing social conditions have modified the traditional pattern somewhat to include single-parent families, two-career families or delayed child-bearing for example, young people still have traditional roles and expectations as guides for their behavior. As they reach adulthood and try to find a place for intimacy in their lives, they can anticipate having a loving relationship and a family of their own.

For gay and lesbian youth these expectations are irrelevant; they don't know how to create something to replace the lost vision of a traditional heterosexual relationship. As there are no set models for gay or lesbian relationships, and few young people have had the chance to meet older gay or lesbian couples, imagining what life will be like is beyond some of them:

> I can't imagine being 65 and still with the same person, but I could imagine being with a man for that long. Long term relationships is [sic] a concept that straights have. I just can't get hold of it. I can't

imagine being older and being with a woman. (lesbian, age 18)

I worry about being alone ten years down the road. I see a lot of young lesbians out there. What happens when you get old? What happens to old lesbians? I don't know. I mean, do they live together and move out to the suburbs or something? (lesbian, age 18)

Young men are particularly pessimistic, because they hear so often that "gay relationships don't last." Some imagine their future filled with a series of casual sexual partners, until they grow old and unattractive and, ultimately, lonely. They are beset by the stereotypical image of the gay couple — the butch and the queen or the young stud and the old man. One service provider notes:

I've met kids whose only experience of gay relationships was from staying up late one night and watching "The Boys in the Band" on TV, or going to see "La Cages aux Folles" ... or girls who found a copy of *The Well of Loneliness*. I even met a girl who had read *The Children's Hour* when she was 13 years old. No wonder these kids get depressed![11]

Young gays and lesbians need to be able to look to their futures with optimism. They need to know that there will be a place in their lives for intimacy. For that to happen, young people must be able to distinguish fact from myth about gay and lesbian relationships. The following discussion will provide some information about gay and lesbian relationships, and a critical evaluation of some of the stereotypes.

Quality of Relationships: Stability and Satisfaction

Gay, lesbian, or straight, each intimate relationship is unique. The values and expectations each partner brings to the relationship, the interactions, and the context in which the relationship exists and grows are different for every couple. These variations make it somewhat difficult but not impossible to generalize about relationships.

Research indicates that there is a higher rate of separation in homosexual relationships than in heterosexual ones (Blumstein & Schwartz, 1983), although many gay and lesbian relationships are long-lasting (Albro & Tully, 1979; Cotton, 1975; Tuller, 1978). The reason for this difference resides not in any inherent inability of homosexuals to form stable relationships, but in the context in which their relationships exist.

The lack of social acceptance is a constant source of stress for lesbian or gay couples in long-term relationships. If the partners are not "out," trying to hide the true nature of the relationship from family, colleagues, and neighbors can be draining. The following comments reflect common experiences:

> We rented a two bedroom apartment because it had to look like we both slept separately. Jill's not out at work, and I'm not out to my parents, and you want to be able to have people over without worrying. (lesbian, age 32)

> My lover had some exploratory surgery because they thought he had cancer. I would have liked to explain to people at work so that they would know why I had seemed irritable or edgy or worried. But I couldn't. Then we worried about whether his parents would honor the will if something happened to him. Then we worried about whether the hospital would let me into intensive care to see him if he ended up there, since I'm not a member of the official immediate family. As it turned out, everything was OK. But his sickness made us feel more vulnerable as a gay couple than we'd ever been. (gay man, age 38)

> Christmas is a very difficult time. Pat spends it with her family and I spend it with mine. We have Christmas on December 27 but it's really not the same. I guess we could come out to them. But it would just be the same. I'm sure my parents wouldn't want my lesbian lover in their home. (lesbian, age 28)

Most heterosexual couples can take for granted the external validation of their relationship. This is not so for the gay or lesbian couple. This includes the legal option to marry as well as social support from co-workers, friends and family (Kurdek & Schmitt, 1987). Sometimes the validation is missing even within the homosexual community where the myth prevails that gay and lesbian relationships don't last. Many homosexual couples live with a general feeling of impermanence. Consequently they are less likely to have joint financial arrangements such as mutually beneficial wills and life insurance or joint bank accounts (Schneider, 1986; Tanner, 1978).

Ironically these are precisely the options for mutual participation which can give a gay or lesbian couple a greater feeling of commitment and legitimacy in the absence of traditional symbols (Dailey, 1977). Thus, when the going gets rough, as can happen in any relationship, the legal and religious supports which may help a heterosexual couple weather the storm are absent for the gay or lesbian couple. Even counselling is less available to homosexuals since some therapists are unwilling to counsel gay or lesbian couples.

The factors which influence permanence also combine to provide greater flexibility for the homosexual couple. In the absence of trappings and formalities, relationships can be established more quickly, and can be dissolved more easily if they no longer meet the needs of the individuals. The unique circumstances under which the homosexual relationship exists can work for or against the couple. It is a challenge to those individuals who seek long term relationships to use the flexibility to their advantage, and to struggle with the absence of supports. The bottom line for couples is that their relationships can endure, although they may have to work harder at it than straight couples, all else being equal.

The quality of homosexual relationships has been compared to that of heterosexual relationships. Studies investigating variables including general satisfaction, degree and magnitude of problems, closeness, marital adjustment, permanence, equality, and interdependence (Dailey, 1979; Peplau, 1981; Schneider, 1986) have found the quality to be remarkably similar. It seems that in spite of the unique stresses on the homosexual couple, the relationships can be as happy and fulfilling as heterosexual relationships.[12]

The research which has been cited here debunks the myth of the unhappy, unstable homosexual relationship. However, the research itself embodies some unspoken biases which ought to be examined. In most of the research, particularly that investigating quality of relationships, the heterosexual relationship is taken implicitly as the baseline or the norm. Expressed in the vernacular, the research question is, "How do homosexual relationships stack up against heterosexual relationships?"

Carried a step further, the research seems to imply that homosexual relationships ought to emulate the traditional heterosexual marriage. Aside from the fact, apparent in the rising divorce rate, that the ideal marriage is at best hard to find, traditional marriage may not be the most appropriate model for a same-sex couple.

Young people questioning their future can be assured that being gay or lesbian will be no barrier to establishing a fulfilling, committed relationship, if that is what they want. They should also know that they have the flexibility to pursue non-traditional forms of relationships if they so choose.

The issue of promiscuity

Homosexuals, particularly men, have long been associated with promiscuity and an over-involvement in matters sexual.[13] They have also been marked as child molesters and seducers of heterosexuals.

These stereotypes have multiple origins. The term "homosexual" itself focusses an inordinate amount of attention on the sexuality of an individual. Furthermore, as explained by Damien Martin in Chapter 7 it is the nature of prejudice that all stigmatized minorities are accused of sexual misconduct, particularly involving children. Homosexuals may be doubly vulnerable to this accusation because their stigmatization revolves around sexuality.

Ironically, the stigmatization itself leads to some of the very behavior which fuels the stereotype of sexual excess. For example, in *Tearoom Trade* by Laud Humphries (1970), an investigation of sex in public washrooms, it was found that approximately 20% of the men engaging in this activity were closeted homosexuals. (Approximately 40% were married heterosexual men for whom washroom sex was their most frequent sexual outlet.) This clandestine sexual activity is the only outlet for sexual expression which these gay men perceive to be available.

Homosexuality comes to public attention most often in connection with something to do with sexual activity — bathhouse raids, male prostitution, arrests for sex in washrooms, and, most recently, the spread of AIDS, a sexually transmitted disease. These items are sensationalized in the news, while the ordinary events in the lives of most homosexuals naturally go unnoticed by the heterosexual population. Again, this type of publicity focusses attention on promiscuous sexual behavior which is in fact characteristic of only a portion of the homosexual population (just as the use of female prostitutes is characteristic of only a portion of heterosexual men).

The type of reporting also biases perceptions of homosexuals. When a man molests a boy he is referred to as a homosexual pedophile. When a man molests a girl he is not called a heterosexual pedophile (nor do we read about a heterosexual rape when a woman is sexually assaulted). In other words, when a sex crime is committed, the term "homosexual" is more likely to be paired with the name of the offence than the term "heterosexual". This gives the public a falsely inflated sense of the frequency with which such crimes are committed by homosexuals as opposed to heterosexuals. This is similar to the practice of reporting the race of an individual who has been accused of a crime when they are non-white, but not when the suspect is white; the result in each instance is that the public's fears and prejudices are reinforced.

It is true, however, that gay men in general tend to lead a more sexually active life than either lesbians or heterosexuals. For example in a large-scale comparison of heterosexual and homosexual cohabiting couples, Blumstein and Schwartz (1983) found that monogamy in relationships is least important to gay men in comparison to heterosexuals and lesbians. In addition, gay men had the highest incidence of non-monogamy in relationships as well as the highest number of sex partners outside the primary relationship.

The reasons for the findings in the study have less to do with homosexuality and more to do with male sexuality in general. As a result of socialization, males seem more able to separate the recreational components of sex from the emotional components, and are more able than are women to enjoy casual, recreational sexual activity. In contrast, women have been socialized to equate sex with emotional involvement. In addition, women have been socialized to say "no" to sex, especially casual sex. The higher rate of monogamy in both heterosexual and lesbian couples is, in part, due to the influence of the female's values. In gay male couples, where both partners can enjoy casual sex and have been socialized to be the pursuer in sexual relationships, the result is almost inevitable.

There are two important things to remember about all relationships, heterosexual or homosexual: (a) They need to be understood and evaluated by taking into account the social context in which they exist; and (b) In spite of valid generalizations, the nature and quality of relationships can vary widely. For example, non-monogamous heterosexual relationships do exist, as do monogamous gay male relationships.

The truth is that generalizing about homosexuals is like generalizing about heterosexuals. What is known about gay and lesbian sexual activity is derived from a relatively visible, and relatively youthful sample, and may not be representative of the entire population. The sexual activities of both heterosexual and homosexual individuals range from celibacy to casual, recreational sex, and are ultimately a matter of personal choice.

If generalizations can be made at all, they apply to male/female, rather than homosexual/heterosexual distinctions. In terms of expectations of relationships and sexual activity, lesbians have more in common with straight women than with gay men. Similarly, gay men have more in common with straight men than with lesbians. In fact, what is observed in the phenomena of gay male sexuality (including gay bathhouses, explicit personal ads in gay publications and the preference for nonmonogamy) is a demonstration of the facility with which men in general can separate the emotional from the recreational components of sex. It might be extrapolated that this is the way some straight men would conduct themselves if they did not have to compromise in relationships with women.

Conclusion

As gay and lesbian adolescents look to the future, they can be reassured that their homosexuality itself will not prevent them from finding a relationship which meets their expectations and fulfills their hopes. They should be aware that they have choices with regard to relationships, sexual activity and the lifestyle they lead.[14]

CHAPTER 5

Attitudes and Beliefs

Nearly everyone, gay or straight, has grown up hearing and believing the myths, stereotypes, and negative attributions associated with homosexuality. These beliefs persist because there is little opportunity and perhaps little motivation to evaluate them critically.

When a friend, client, colleague, or family member openly identifies him/herself as gay or lesbian, individuals are challenged to examine their attitudes and beliefs. Such self-examination may uncover a confusing and perplexing mixture of feelings and thoughts, regarding not only homosexuality *per se*, but also sexuality in general, appropriate sex roles, family, and social structures.

Often, people have mixed reactions to homosexuality. While they may be willing intellectually to accept that it is simply a variation of sexual development, on a gut level they wonder whether homosexuals aren't really sick or sinful. When confronted with the reality of a gay or lesbian client, friend, or family member, people may wonder how to cope with their contradictory feelings. Social service providers may be concerned that such feelings, if they exist, might affect their work with gay or lesbian clients. They may wish to examine and modify their feelings. This section addresses some of these concerns. It begins with an explanation of the foundations of homophobia, discusses the ways in which homophobia can be manifested, and suggests approaches to modifying homophobia.

Homophobia Defined and Examined

Homophobia is the term used to describe extreme, negative attitudes, feelings, and beliefs regarding homosexuality; it is also used loosely to refer to any degree of negativity toward homosexuality. Thus, homophobia can range from hatred and extreme fear of homosexuals to feelings of disquiet or discomfort. The term "phobia" stresses the irrational component of these feelings. Homophobia is comparable in some ways to disproportionate fear of snakes, heights, elevators, and the like. The extent of homophobia in North America is reflected by research findings which indicate that homosexuals are more stigmatized than drug addicts, alcoholics, criminals, and members of those racial minorities that are customarily subject to discrimination (Corbett, Troiden, & Dodder, 1977). Parents have been heard to say, upon learning that their child is gay or lesbian, that they would have preferred to hear that their child was a murderer or had cancer.

Like all attitudes and beliefs, homophobia is learned. It varies in nature and degree depending on individuals and cultures and is characterized by a mixture of commonly held notions which include the following:

1) Homosexuals are fundamentally different from heterosexuals.
2) Homosexuals hate and fear the opposite sex.
3) Homosexuals act like the opposite sex, and want to be the opposite sex.
4) Homosexuals are excessively sexual.
5) Homosexuals are threats to others. They prey on heterosexual adults and children for sexual gratification and for the purposes of recruiting heterosexuals.
6) Homosexuals are failures. They turn to the same sex because they cannot find or maintain relationships with the opposite sex.
7) Homosexuals and their relationships are neurotic and unstable.

These beliefs have no foundation in fact, yet they persist in spite of substantial evidence to the contrary. For example, some participants in workshops on homophobia say that they would be concerned if their child's elementary school teacher were a gay man. They would fear that their child might be molested sexually. Participants continue to express concern even after learning of research data which clearly indicate that both boys and girls are more likely to be molested by heterosexual males (Newton, 1978). With similar tenacity, some workshop participants cling to the stereotypical image of lesbians and gay men. When they are shown videotapes of non-stereotypical lesbians and gays, or when they meet non-stereotypical individuals in person some participants dismiss these individuals as exceptions to the rule.

To begin understanding the irrational persistence of homophobia, the next section examines its possible foundation.

The Roots of Homophobia

The roots of prejudice in general, and homophobia in particular, are too complex to examine fully in this discussion; yet the similarities between homophobia and racism are too conspicuous to ignore. (This is why some exercises promoting awareness of racial discrimination are often modified and used in staff-training exercises designed to examine homophobia.) When a minority group is stigmatized, be it blacks, Jews, Catholics, or others, specific beliefs emerge repeatedly as justification for discrimination. As Damien Martin points out in Chapter 7, historically, minorities have been portrayed as sexually uncontrolled, and preying on women and children. They have been perceived as threats to society, with the fear that if minority members were allowed to mingle with the majority, or extended equal rights (often misinterpreted as meaning special privileges) the minority would contaminate and eventually overpower the dominant group. These beliefs are buttressed by the notion that minorities are essentially different from the majority (Martin, 1982). The similarity of attitudes and beliefs regarding homosexuals and other minorities suggest that they are the justification for, not the cause of, homophobia. In fact, the cause is rooted in a far deeper hostility and fear.

Fear of gender-role deviance is the most compelling factor explaining homophobia. Research findings indicate that rigid gender-role stereotyping (i.e. sexism) is the one constant among homophobic individuals (Henley & Pincus, 1978; McDonald & Games, 1974; Minnigerode, 1976). The fear is that the family will be undermined, and society undone, if men and women meld their roles.

The family, as we know it, is the cornerstone of social order, and is founded on the heterosexual relationship which embodies these roles. Any deviation from prescribed gender roles is thus perceived as a threat to the social fabric of society. Same-sex erotic attraction, which is the essence of homosexuality, is gender-role deviant because traditionally individuals are supposed to have sex only with members of the opposite sex. Homosexuality, like feminism, challenges the social order in Western culture, which rests on role differentiation between males and females, in particular on the unequal division of power and status which confers privilege and advantage to males. Homosexuality, then, is a threat of the most elemental sort. This goes far in explaining the entrenchment of homophobia on a cultural and societal level.

Research investigating individual differences in degree of homophobia has revealed that negative attitudes are associated with a general conservatism, that is, a general resistance to social change. Homophobia is more likely to be found in those who are older and not well-educated (Herek, 1984), in those who espouse conservative religious ideologies (Herek, 1984), and in those who tend to be restrictive regarding all sexual activity (McDonald & Games, 1974; Minnigerode, 1976).

Homophobic individuals tend to be rigid in their thinking, inflexible, are likely to be authoritarian and have a low tolerance for ambiguity (McDonald & Games, 1974). They tend to be status conscious (Smith, 1971), and, as mentioned earlier, adhere to clearly and narrowly defined gender roles and behavior (McDonald & Games, 1974; Minnigerode, 1974; Laner & Laner, 1980). This research suggests that extreme homophobia may be very resistant to change, and that any examination of attitudes and beliefs must be preceded by an openness to change.

The Effects of Homophobia on Counselling Practice

Social service professionals are normally well-versed in the importance of acceptance; they are not, however, necessarily immune to homophobic beliefs and attitudes (Davison & Wilson, 1973; Schneider & Tremble, 1985; Steffenmeier & Steffenmeier, 1978). The way in which these attitudes and beliefs may affect clients is a particular concern for workers.

The effect of homophobia on clinical judgments was demonstrated recently by the comments of a psychiatrist attending a workshop about lesbian and gay youth. Participants had just finished watching a videotape of parents of gay and lesbian youth discussing how they had successfully come to terms with their children's sexual orientation (Tremble & Central Toronto Youth Services, 1985). The psychiatrist, who described himself as being comfortable with gay and lesbian clients, questioned whether adolescents should come out to their parents at all. He argued that it could only hurt the parents, especially since it was obviously the parents' fault that the child was homosexual. Furthermore, he believed that if the parents hadn't already acknowledged to themselves that their child was homosexual, they were obviously repressing the knowledge because they did not want to hear it.

This professional who readily acknowledged the value of bringing family secrets (such as alcoholism or incest) out into the open, was advocating that a family collude to keep the child's sexuality a secret. He also indicated by his comment that, in spite of the evidence presented in the videotape, he could not envision the parents ever coming to terms with the issue or that the family unit might be healthier once the initial crisis had passed. Finally, by placing blame on the parents he was implying that there was something essentially wrong with homosexuality (since blame is attributed only when something is wrong). The most disturbing aspect of his comments was his inability to perceive his own negativity about homosexuality which had become apparent to the entire group in the workshop. One might wonder how this negativity is reflected in his work with gay and lesbian clients.

Experimental research has shown that attitudes do translate into behavior. Research participants in experimental settings tend to evaluate homosexuals more negatively than they do heterosexuals, in a variety of areas of functioning, everything else being equal (Krulewitz & Nash, 1980; San Miguel & Millham, 1976). They tend to maintain a greater personal distance from homosexuals (for example they will sit further away) than from heterosexuals, and will avoid working with homosexuals when possible (Karr, 1981; Krulewitz & Nash, 1980; Morin, Taylor & Kielman, 1975). This research suggests that negative attitudes can be conveyed subtly to gay or lesbian clients, and that professional objectivity can be impaired by negative attitudes.

The results of survey research indicate that many helping professionals believe in the stereotypical image of gay males and lesbians. For example, a survey of over 300 social service providers revealed that 32% believed that gay males are more feminine than heterosexual males, while 24% believed that lesbians are more masculine than heterosexual women. Twenty-four percent believed that they could identify homosexuals by their appearance and speech and 21% believed that homosexuals were more likely than heterosexuals to abuse children sexually (Schneider & Tremble, 1985). Such stereotyped beliefs are manifested in statements such as "but she didn't look like a lesbian" or "but gay men shouldn't work in child care." These beliefs limit workers in their ability to identify clients for whom sexual orientation is an issue and to help their clients plan for the future.

Effective service provision for gay and lesbian youth requires the same things that service for other minority clients requires — a sensitivity to the uniqueness of the client's situation combined with a sense of the client's commonality with other clients. Service providers need to develop a positive attitude toward homosexuality and to understand what it really means to be gay or lesbian. What is required is willingness to examine one's own attitudes and beliefs, openness to changing belief systems which are deeply rooted in most people, and the opportunity to explore attitudes and obtain accurate information, ideally through staff-training programs. These are the conditions under which service providers can become gay-affirmative, that is,

> exploring options available to gay/lesbian clients, [able to assist] in developing a self-affirming lifestyle and works [sic] on general life issues without necessarily attributing them to the client's [sexual orientation]. (Douce, 1985, p. 3)

The steps which workers can take in order to develop a gay-affirmative attitude are discussed in the next section.

Dealing with Discomfort

Two options exist for workers who experience some discomfort with homosexuality. In the interests of both sound social work practice as well as personal growth, workers may decide to examine their biases and take steps to become more comfortable. (Some ways of doing this will be discussed later.) Those who are convinced that homosexuality is immoral, sick, or second-best may have little interest in changing. The issue for these workers is the effect of their condemnation on the lesbian or gay client, and whether or not they should be working with these clients at all.

Mental health professionals often feel that they must be all things to all people. However, just as people with an anti-abortion stance could not be expected to do their best work with women who have elected to have an abortion, it is unlikely that those with objections to homosexuality will do their most effective work with young gays and lesbians. Professionals need to give themselves and one another permission to choose where they can be most productive. For the good of all concerned, workers who have difficulty accepting homosexuality should choose to work only with heterosexual clients.

Sometimes that is not an option. Workers may be assigned a lesbian or gay client arbitrarily or they may establish a solid relationship with a client who discloses after six months that s/he is lesbian or gay. In these instances, workers may be obliged to examine and modify their attitudes and beliefs.

The process can begin with collecting information. The material in the bibliography at the back of this book can be found at public libraries or can be ordered through local bookstores. A local gay or lesbian organization may be able to provide information or training workshops. Gay or lesbian colleagues may be willing and able to act as resources. If there are no resources available locally, human resources from another location may be approached to conduct training sessions locally.

Meeting gay and lesbian individuals is another part of the process. Gays and lesbians become ordinary, non-threatening people when the theoretical becomes concrete.

The process of self-examination requires that individuals listen closely to what they themselves feel, think, and say. Overtly homophobic statements and feelings are easy to identify, but the subtle indicators of homophobia are more difficult to recognize. The following are a few examples:

1. *Qualifying statements.* Comments such as, "Homosexuals are OK as long as ..." indicate negativity in some form. For example, "... as long as they don't come on to me," implies a belief in the stereotypical notion that homosexuals are interested in seducing heterosexuals, and, further, that unwanted homosexual advances are worse than unwanted heterosexual advances.

2. *Double standards.* Applying double standards in judging behavior is indicative of discomfort with homosexuality. For example, it is considered appropriate for heterosexuals to talk about celebrating an anniversary with a spouse, or going dancing at a local club. However, when homosexuals mention celebrating with a lover or going to a dance at the gay community center it is called flaunting their sexuality.

3. *Expecting exemplary behavior.* A growing awareness of racial issues has made apparent the racist overtones in a statement like, "She is a credit to her race." Similarly, when gays and lesbians are always expected to be model citizens (according to whose model?) so as not to sully the reputation of all homosexuals, the underlying prejudice needs to be recognized.

4. *Value judgments.* Statements such as those which follow contain implicit value judgments about particular behaviors:
"Lesbians shouldn't make radical feminist statements because then it seems like all lesbians hate men." "Gay men are only hurting their own reputations when they put graphic ads in the personal columns." These reflect the speaker's idea of appropriate behavior and deny the right of gays and lesbians to choose how they will behave. Here again there is an inherent double standard in these statements; no one would suggest that heterosexual men stop placing explicit ads in personal columns on the grounds it gives all heterosexual men a bad name.

[handwritten marginal note: LIBERTARIAN AGENDA]

[handwritten marginal note: NO??]

These examples illustrate a few of the less overt ways in which negative attitudes manifest themselves. Ironically, such statements are mistakenly thought to be gay-positive. Sometimes a trained facilitator or resource person is needed to assist people in recognizing and unravelling their underlying attitudes and beliefs about homosexuality so that they can modify them.

Helping professionals have a responsibility to ensure that personal biases do not impair their work. This means developing a gay-affirmative stance, and examining the attitudes and beliefs of a lifetime, recognizing that they may be difficult to change. No one should be blamed for feeling discomfort with the issues of homosexuality as long as they are willing to examine these feelings in an open and honest way. Based on such an examination they can then decide whether they are the appropriate people to work with gay and lesbian clients.

CHAPTER 6

Adolescent Development and the Coming-Out Process

In a world in which all are assumed to be, and all assume themselves to be, heterosexual, how individuals determine that they are homosexual is a fascinating question. The process is called "coming out," and is defined as "the developmental process through which gay people recognize their sexual preferences and choose to integrate this knowledge into their personal and social lives" (De Monteflores & Schultz, 1978, p. 59).

Coming out involves five interrelated areas of development: (a) the growing awareness of homosexual feelings and identity; (b) developing intimate same-sex romantic/erotic relationships; (c) developing social ties with gay and lesbian peers or community; (d) developing a positive evaluation of homosexuality; and (e) self-disclosure.

always in this order?

Many gay men and lesbians describe coming out as a life-long process. Closure is achieved finally when sexual orientation is appropriately placed in perspective relative to the individual's overall identity, when friendships and intimate relationships are established with gay and lesbian peers and when gay-positive feelings develop. All of this takes place of course in the larger context of general life issues. For adolescents, the tasks of coming out are closely related to the developmental issues faced by all adolescents. For example, developing social ties with gay and lesbian peers is part of establishing a community of friends, gay or straight, through work, leisure activity or in the neighborhood; self-disclosure is part of the larger issue of delineating boundaries between the private and public aspects of one's life.

The coming-out process is an individual experience. The milestones, the hurdles and the pace of the process, all vary from person to person. Individuals bring a variety of coping skills, problem-solving abilities and resources to the process, just as they would to any life crisis. Consequently, some people move through the process relatively smoothly, accepting their sexuality, making social contacts and so on, while others are horrified by their sexuality, painfully vacillating in their determination and floundering in their attempts to find a peer group.

Three general patterns of coming out emerge from the variety of individual experiences. Some people have a sense of always having been gay or lesbian; their growing awareness of sexual and affectional feelings was always homosexual. Others switch rather abruptly from a heterosexual to a homosexual orientation in adulthood, usually as the result of falling in love with a particular person (this appears to be an almost exclusively female phenomenon). Still others vacillate between a heterosexual and homosexual orientation until arriving at a determination, often after adolescence (Eisner, 1982).

At the best of times, coming out is stressful; it is especially so for gay and lesbian adolescents. First, they are becoming aware of being different and feeling alienated at a time when being like everyone else is very important. Second, they are particularly vulnerable due to their emotional and financial dependence on parents and their obligation to attend school. As adolescents, their coping skills are not fully elaborated, and the stresses induced by the coming-out process compound the existing demands of the developmental tasks they face. Because of their age and lack of mobility, youngsters can make only limited use, if any, of the resources within the gay of lesbian community. Thus, they remain particularly isolated during the coming-out process.

The tasks of coming out parallel the major developmental tasks of all adolescents, which include establishing a sense of identity, developing self-esteem, learning the social skills necessary for maintaining friendships, and, in the context of a growing sexual awareness, finding meaning and a place in life for intimacy. Coming out adds a new dimension to these tasks.

Identity

Adolescence is a time for identity consolidation (Erikson, 1963), for answering the question, "Who am I?" The gay or lesbian adolescent must also ask, "What does it mean to be gay?" That is a difficult question to answer. Beyond the characteristic same-sex attraction, being homosexual holds diverse meaning for different individuals (Eisner, 1982; Golden, 1987). Despite research attesting to the diversity of the gay and lesbian population, the myths and stereotypes of the unstable, gender inappropriate, and lecherous homosexual persist. Most gay or lesbian adolescents have met few, if any, admitted homosexuals. They have had little opportunity to examine these myths and stereotypes critically. Lacking insight into the variability of the homosexual population, a gay or lesbian youngster may attempt to act out the stereotype in the erroneous belief that this is the only way to be homosexual. As one young woman explained:

> When I finally decided that I was a lesbian, I decided to be the best lesbian you'd ever seen. So I started wearing plaid flannel shirts, blue jeans, and work boots, until I got used to my lesbian identity. Then I started dressing like myself again.

This phase is relatively harmless for most young people, and the behavior subsides as identity issues are resolved. However, adolescents with a tendency to act out extravagantly, or exhibit a pattern of self-destruction, may be at risk. Some gay males may use the image of the hustler as an excuse to opt out of the responsibilities of growing up. Other youngsters simply believe that hustling is what the "gay lifestyle" is all about, and they see themselves, when they are too old to hustle, as the men who drive around the block looking for sex. Some youngsters may victimize themselves by acting out the flagrantly effeminate gay male image, or playing the part of the "butch" lesbian, leaving themselves open to the verbal and physical abuse of their straight peers. Assaults against homosexuals are rarely invited and never excusable. However, self-destructive young people may use sexual orientation in this way to evoke negative reactions.

Often the characteristic "gay" or "lesbian" is allowed to obscure all the other important attributes of the individual. This is a major pitfall for adolescents who are coming out, as well as for the people surrounding them. For most people, gay or straight, sexual orientation is not the most salient part of their identity and sexual behavior is not their most noteworthy activity. Knowing that someone is gay or lesbian tells you no more than knowing that someone is straight. Knowing that a person skiis, hikes or reads science fiction is more informative. The task for the young gay or lesbian individual is to put sexual orientation into an appropriate perspective. However, what constitutes "appropriate" is an individual judgment, likely approximating Cass's (1979) definition of identity synthesis:

> With the development process completed, homosexual identity is integrated with all other aspects of self. Instead of being seen as *the*

identity, it is now given the status of being merely one aspect of self. (p. 235)

The task of placing sexual orientation into perspective faces anyone working or associating with young gay males or lesbians. The tendency in society is to focus on the single most noteworthy attribute of anyone who is different from us in a particularly obvious way, even when that attribute is not necessarily germane to one's relationship with that individual. This is seen when people encounter someone in a wheelchair, or a person from a different racial or ethnic background, assuming that the obvious character-istic is the most relevant. An individual is perceived as a black person who hikes, a Moslem who reads science fiction, or a lesbian who skiis, rather than as a hiker, science fiction buff, or a skiier. While in some contexts, reference to these characteristics is appropriate, more often than not it is irrelevant.

Self-esteem

Many gay and lesbian adolescents lack self esteem. This is understandable in a world which tells youngsters that homosexuality is a crime, a sin, or an illness. As one young man commented, "I thought I was essentially a bad person because I was gay." Stereotypes such as those discussed in Chapter 2 often exacerbate the youngster's feelings of deficiency. Without self-esteem, adolescents have difficulty feeling good about anything they do, whether in school, at home, or in social situations. Planning for the future becomes difficult since the future looks so bleak.

As young gay men and lesbians begin to accept and feel positive about their sexuality, however, other areas of their lives start to come together.

> I no longer felt awful because I was attracted to men. It's incredible how many other things hinged on the resolution of that conflict. When I cleared up not accepting myself as a homosexual, everything else hinged on that, like confidence in myself. (gay male, age 20)

and:

> I changed my choice of career ... I could have done pretty well in accounting but ... I decided to make a change and get into film. I think that was based on the new freedom I felt [when I came out]. It changed my life. (lesbian, age 19)

> My sexuality was a piece of my life that I had denied for a long time, and suddenly you allow yourself to fit that piece in with the rest of the pieces. In that sense, when I finally felt OK about being a lesbian, I felt

much more like a whole person. (lesbian, age 19)

Conversely, success in other areas of life facilitates the development of gay-positive feelings. For example, one young woman related how she had tried to repress and deny her homosexual feelings throughout her teens, experiencing frequent bouts of anxiety and depression as a result. In her early twenties, she enrolled in a couple of part-time university courses and did very well. That gave her the confidence to acknowledge and explore her sexuality for the first time, and eventually come to accept herself as a lesbian (Eisner, 1982).

In order for young people to develop a positive homosexual identity, it is essential that they are exposed to positive gay and lesbian role models — both peer and adult. Adolescents need to see people whose lifestyles demonstrate that being gay or lesbian is not a barrier to being happy, productive, and respected by peers. They need to see that the negative stereotype of the homosexual is far removed from reality. They need to know that other people, who are like them, have the same kinds of feelings. For many gay and lesbian youngsters, meeting peers and older adults, particularly adults in committed, long-term relationships, is a milestone in accepting their own sexuality and validating their feelings.

> I hadn't met any lesbians up 'til then. I knew they were somewhere, but I felt isolated. Then I got involved with this lesbian group on campus and I realized that these women were feeling the same things that I felt and what I'd been reading about lesbians was, in fact, about me. (lesbian, age 22)

> When you find friends who are supportive, not only supportive, but in the same boat as you, and you can see for yourself that their life isn't hell and that a lot of things you hear about gay lifestyle and gay people isn't true, you find there's nothing really different about them, then you think, gee, it's OK. (gay male, age 22)

Supportive heterosexual role models are equally important for gay and lesbian youngsters. Acceptance and understanding from a straight adult is especially important.

Socialization

Most lesbian and gay adolescents have heterosexual friends. They may "date" heterosexually in response to peer or parental pressure, out of social necessity such as a high school dance, and out of a desire to "fit in." However, they have little or no opportunity to meet and socialize with lesbian or gay peers, and as a consequence are often deprived of some important adolescent experiences. These include (a) learning the social conventions of dating same-sex partners, (b) having romantic experiences of adolescence, and (c) experimenting sexually. Consequently they experience a developmental lag (Maylon, 1982) in that they do not experience adolescence fully until their late teens and early twenties after they have left high school and come into contact with gay and lesbian peers for the first time.

Some lesbian and gay adolescents do find their way to the visible gay and lesbian communities. Frequently these youngsters socialize in the adult-focussed environment of the bars and clubs. Although most of these adolescents find these to be exciting places to go, many will admit that they really do not belong there (Schneider, in press). Furthermore, by socializing outside of their own neighborhoods they do not have the security of the socially sanctioned context in which most heterosexual adolescents develop their social awareness.

Gay male adolescents may be particularly at risk because of the opportunities for casual, anonymous sex in some segments of the gay community. Young men may seek the "cruising areas" in the city looking for sexual experience. It is sad that this seems to them to be the only way to find a meaningful personal contact with other gay males. Most often, all they find is a hasty sexual encounter.

Young lesbians are less likely than gay young men to come in contact with the lesbian or gay community partly because of more stringent parental restrictions on the freedom of young women in general to come and go without explanation. However, young lesbians are more likely to find an intimate long-term sexual relationship. Problems can arise when the relationship, existing in isolation, becomes too enmeshed and the partners too dependent. Joyce Hunter, Director of Social Services at the Hetrick-Martin Institute in New York has noted several instances in which young lesbians in these relationships have great difficulty separating themselves psychologically from each other, especially when they eventually do meet other lesbians.

Whether or not they are isolated from homosexual peers, the socializing experiences of lesbian and gay youth are different from and, in many ways, more stressful than they are for their heterosexual counterparts. The sources of stress will be discussed in the following section.

Stress and the Gay or Lesbian Adolescent

At a time when heterosexual adolescents are learning how to socialize, [young gay and lesbian people] are learning to hide. (Hetrick & Martin, 1983, p.6)

The complexities of adolescent development for gay or lesbian youth create a dimension of stress in their lives not experienced by straight adolescents. This stress manifests itself in the day-to-day lives of these adolescents.

While most young people have a feeling that they are different from everyone else, for homosexual youngsters that sense of differentness increases as they become aware of their attraction to the same sex. This is compounded by the fact that they seldom have anyone in whom to confide. As heterosexual peers begin to date and experiment sexually, the homosexual youth's sense of difference is accentuated. Consequently, the homosexual youth may withdraw from this type of socializing, or try to fit in by going through the motions. Feigning heterosexual interest often generates a feeling of dishonesty, artificiality, and sometimes, panic at the thought of having to perform sexually.

Some youngsters try and make themselves "go straight" by repressing their same-sex feelings. Sometimes, inadvertently, many other feelings are repressed as well. Predictably, some of them experience severe anxiety and depression. When these young people finally admit the truth to themselves, they often regain a sense of openness and freedom to be themselves.

In the effort to "go straight" some adolescents will engage in compulsive heterosexual behavior. Young men may masturbate frequently while looking at pictures of nude women, while young women may have sex with many different male partners, sometimes resulting in pregnancy. All this is undertaken in the hope that the activity will awaken heterosexual desire. Ultimately, such attempts are unsuccessful and only contribute to the person's growing sense of failure, alienation, and loneliness.

Uncomfortable encounters in everyday life add to their pain. Anti-homosexual jokes, crude remarks about queers and dykes, and the ultimate put-down, "That's gay!" are like minefields as youngsters struggle to react without giving their sexuality away. Even adolescents who characteristically would react to racial or ethnic slurs by commenting on the racism feel paralyzed and unable to respond.

Adolescents of both sexes have problems if they are perceived to be gender-atypical. However, peers, teachers, and parents are likely to dismiss girls as going through a tomboy phase, while there is no such discounting young men's behavior.

Young men perceived to be effeminate may be harassed by their heterosexual peers. Young people have described being teased, baited, and beaten up, particularly at school (Heron, 1983; Patterson, 1985). Often, little, if any, support is forthcoming from school officials who feel ill-prepared or are simply unwilling to intervene. Some youngsters stick it out. Others leave school, their education incomplete.

Unlike other adolescents who encounter difficulty with peers because of race, disability, personal appearance, and so on, lesbian and gay youth usually cannot turn to their families for support. Their families are unaware of their sexual orientation and self-disclosure is not an option. Young gays and lesbians are too emotionally and physically dependent on parents to contend with the inevitable upset which, at least initially, accompanies self-disclosure. Yet, the unspoken secret exacerbates the usual conflicts between adolescents and their parents. Gay and lesbian youngsters frequently describe an undercurrent of things left unsaid in the family as if by tacit agreement. One young man recalled that his mother told him to leave home because she could not abide "his lifestyle," although she never defined exactly what she meant, and the subject of his sexual orientation had never been broached. Although adolescents who disclose are often met with support, more than one young person has been thrown out of the home when parents are told, or inadvertently find out, that the youngster is homosexual.

Most gay and lesbian adolescents are not asked to leave home. However, they do tend to leave, of their own accord, at an earlier age than their heterosexual counterparts (Schneider, 1985). They are often escaping family tensions or seeking the freedom to explore the homosexual community. They tire of painful equivocation when interested parents ask, "Where'd you go?," "What did you do?" or "Who were you with?" Evasion is most hurtful when the family is otherwise close. As one youngster said, "I was always very close with my mother. What hurt the most was not being able to tell her I was gay." As for parents, the growing sense of inexplicable distance becomes cause for concern. As an alternative to disclosure, children leave home, perhaps before they are really ready to take that step toward independence.

Gay and lesbian youth have little room to maneuver, obliged by necessity and the law to remain in school where they often feel like outsiders while, as explained in Chapter 3, the homosexual community offers few places for them. Living with parents can be full of tension. How do these youngsters cope? Some — a minority — cannot. They withdraw, depressed or suicidal (Kournary, 1987; Rofes, 1983). They quit school and leave home. Some are thrown out of their homes with no place to go. For the majority, however, the watershed comes when they leave home for college, university, or the workforce. They can then contact the gay and lesbian community being at an age when they can find a niche there.

Coping with both the complexities of developmental tasks and the stresses of day-to-day living often taxes the energy and attention of the gay or lesbian adolescent in a way that has no parallel in the lives of heterosexual youth. For straight adolescents, sexuality emerges in a relatively predictable and expected way. Lesbian and gay youth not only have to become aware of sexual feelings for which no one prepared them but they also have to construct an entirely new set of expectations for their future. Not uncommonly, the academic interest of these adolescents wanes and their performance suffers. Usually, in their early twenties, developmental issues are resolved, and independence is established. At that time, young gays or lesbians address the future. Many young people backtrack, returning to school or vocational training, and then embark upon a career. While they are doing this somewhat later than their heterosexual peers, they frequently carry with them increased coping skills, the result of having met earlier crises successfully. The necessity of having had to examine their identity, feelings about themselves, and their relationships seems to contribute to a stronger sense of self in these adolescents. In the words of one young woman,

> I decided I was a lesbian when I was very young. Once you've made that decision, it's so big, about what you are and who you are, that there's no obstacle after that. If I could do that then I can do anything. (lesbian, age 19)

Another young person pointed out,

> I have to be a bit stronger because there's [sic] so many people who don't understand. If every time somebody made a crack about queers you got upset, you'd be some kind of a nut. You have to be a little more tolerant and I don't think that's bad. (gay male, age 20)

Summary

The developmental deficits in the lives of lesbian and gay youth cannot be overcome, nor can the issues be resolved, until the adolescent has an opportunity to ascertain the meaning of being gay or lesbian — what it means in terms of identity, self-esteem, and relationships. This cannot be done in isolation. Gay and lesbian peers, adult role models, and/or a homosexual community are necessary as points of reference in the coming-out process. The complex demands of coming out and growing up impose stress and pain on the homosexual adolescent and can take years. Helping to cut the emotional costs is one of the challenges faced by adults who work with these youngsters.

CHAPTER 7

The Stigmatization of the Gay or Lesbian Adolescent

A. Damien Martin

Several of my colleagues were surprised when I mentioned that I was preparing a paper on problems and issues in the delivery of services to gay and lesbian youth. Their recurring comment was, "Why not just treat them like anyone else?" Would that we could do so!

The truth is that gay and lesbian youth are not like other adolescents. Their difference stems from their status as members of one of the most hated and despised minority groups in the country.

Gordon Allport defines the term "minority group" in his classic work *The Nature of Prejudice*: any group that suffers from unjustified negative treatment from the dominant group (Allport, 1958); in other words, any group that falls victim to prejudice.

Granting that gay people are indeed a minority group raises an immediate question. If their difference arises solely from their status as members of a minority group, why not treat them like members of any hated group? Why not just apply what we have learned from working with blacks, or Hispanics? Only to a certain extent is this an appropriate strategy. As shall

Damien Martin is Associate Professor in the Department of Communication Arts and Sciences, School of Education, Health, Nursing, and Arts Professions, New York University, and is Executive Director and co-founder of the Hetrick-Martin Institute (formerly the Institute for the Protection of Lesbian and Gay Youth), New York City.

be discussed below, members of all minority groups often share certain problems that are a direct result of prejudice. Thus, gay and lesbian adolescents often have problems in common with their black and Hispanic counterparts. But each minority group suffers specific exigencies related to their group. For example, black youngsters may suffer from economic deprivation, while the average gay or lesbian white youngster may not. Hispanic youths may suffer from the conflicting values of opposing cultures, while non-Hispanic gay and lesbian youth may not. But gay and lesbian adolescents have special problems, too. Blacks, Jews, and Hispanics are not thrown out of their families or religions at adolescence for being black, Jewish or Hispanic — gay and lesbian kids are. Even more importantly, other minority adolescents, no matter how terrible the social or economic deprivation under which they may exist, have a chance to develop a sense of the "we" versus "they," the very essence of group identity; gay and lesbian kids do not. Instead, for many homosexually oriented people, adolescence is the time when they begin to realize they belong to a group that supposedly can bring about the fall of civilizations, the destruction of the family, the corruption of children, and the betrayal of all our national secrets to blackmailing Russian agents. That does tend to have an effect on a young teenager with no access to correct information; an effect that is seldom positive.

This is not offered as part of the "who has suffered more" argument, which is worthless. Pain is pain no matter who is suffering. The point is that gay and lesbian youth, even though they share many of the fears, attitudes and needs of their heterosexual counterparts, do have special problems that arise not only from their being members of a stigmatized group, but because their group is particularly hated. What is offered is a brief outline of the process by which the gay and lesbian adolescent is stigmatized, an outline that can serve as a conceptual framework for working with these young people. The other articles in this book will address and expand on particulars of the specific problems themselves.

Prejudice

Gay people are members of a minority group because they are the victims of a prejudice. Gordon Allport defines prejudice as a negative categorical attitude based on error and overgeneralization (Allport, 1958). For example: all Jews are communists; all Catholics must vote the way their priest tells them to vote; all blacks are lazy and on welfare; women cannot be effective workers because of menstruation, and so on. One example related to homosexuality is provided by Edmund Bergler, a psychiatrist well known during the "homosexual menace" days of the McCarthy period. He had this to say:

I can say with some justification that I have no bias against homosexuals; for me they are sick people requiring medical help.... Still, though I have no bias, if I were asked what kind of person the homosexual is, I would say: Homosexuals are essentially disagreeable people, regardless of their pleasant or unpleasant outward manner. [Their] shell is a mixture of superciliousness, fake aggression, and whimpering.... They are subservient when confronted with a stronger person, merciless when in power, unscrupulous about trampling on a weaker person. The only language their unconscious understands is brute force (Bergler, 1957, pp. 28-29).

Most would agree that Bergler's comment is negative; Most would also recognize that it is erroneous and an overgeneralization.

If prejudice were only a matter of negative opinions or attitudes, it would not be very important, except perhaps to the person who held it. Everyone is entitled to hold opinions, no matter how stupid or wrong. However, these attitudes are often acted upon with negative consequences for the hated group and for society as well. When prejudice is acted out, it has three stages: antilocutions, discrimination, and finally violence (Allport, 1958).

Antilocutions are the rhetoric of prejudice, the negative verbal statements and beliefs about the hated group. Antilocutions can range from derogatory and trivializing terms — kike, nigger, spic, faggot or dyke — to elaborate "scientific" theories designed to demonstrate the inferiority or danger of the group. Most people forget that racism was an accepted and respectable scientific theory during the nineteenth century.

Antilocutions about gay people cover quite a range. The following is just a sampling of the kinds of beliefs and attitudes promulgated in a number of contexts. Dr. Harold Voth, a psychiatrist at the Menninger Clinic, in the United States, wrote this about gay people:

Homosexuality is as much a public health problem as any of the major diseases which have concerned public officials and the medical profession. It is contrary to nature.... Little good can come to children from exposure to adults who are so disturbed as to become overtly homosexual (Voth, 1977, p.83).

Dr. Voth offers no evidence to support his contentions. His libel is prototypical in that it exhibits two of the major accusations usually brought against any minority group but especially against gay people: that the group is a health hazard and, that the group poses a special danger to children. Both themes occur repeatedly in the rhetoric of prejudice. Hitler and other Nazis parroted the metaphor of the Jew as a virus or germ and proposed "radical treatment." They also painted Jews as corrupters of children and even went so far as to accuse them of ritual murder of Christian babies. Gypsies supposedly kidnapped babies and, in our own country, blacks were considered so dangerous and corrupting that in the United States they were not allowed to go to school with white youngsters.

These same themes run through most anti-gay rhetoric. A Jesuit priest, Father Herbert Smith, and a psychiatrist who teaches creative arts therapy, Dr. Joseph Dilenno, offer this gem in a recent book:

> Most normal people hate and fear homosexual practices both because they fear their own passions, and because they are afraid for their own children.... Their fears are not empty. Besides being unnatural and sterile, homosexual acts are a contagious cause of tragedy, and destructive of the natural relationships between the sexes. For heterosexuals by the abuse of sex — by moral contagion, and by seduction and rape. There are thousands of young boys in large American cities whose services have literally been bought by active homosexuals. It is for these reasons that religious and civil authorities oppose active homosexuality (Smith and Dilenno, 1979, pp. 50-51).

Needless to say, Father Smith and Dr. Dilenno do not mention the many more thousands of young girls "whose services have literally been bought by active" heterosexuals. In this they resemble Thomas Aquinas who taught that heterosexual rape and incest are preferable to homosexuality because rape and incest are more "natural."

Anti-gay attacks do not come solely from the Church and the medical establishment, however. Joseph Epstein, a self-described liberal and fighter for civil rights, wrote the following for Harper's a few years back:

> They are different from the rest of us. Homosexuals are different, moreover, in a way that cuts deeper than other kinds of human differences — religious, class, racial, in a way that is, somehow more fundamental. Cursed without clear cause, afflicted without apparent cure, they are an affront to our rationality ... there is much that my four sons can do in their lives that might cause me anguish, that might outrage me, that might make me ashamed of them and myself as their father. But nothing they could ever do would make me sadder than if any of them were to become homosexual (Epstein, 1970, pp. 36-51).

In other words, for this father, to be homosexual is worse than being a murderer, a rapist, a drug pusher or an addict. One can only wonder about how a son of Mr. Epstein who was homosexual would have felt. How would he have viewed himself? How would he have felt about talking to his father about himself? Could he have spoken to his father or been at all open in his life with his family?

Mr. Epstein's fear and hatred of gay people are not uncommon, and these feelings have an unfortunate effect on gay children. Most workers in the field have had to deal with those youngsters, barely into their teens, who have been beaten by their parents and thrown out into the street to survive as best they can, solely because the parents discovered the child was homosexually oriented. Such parental reactions should not be surprising. Like others in our society, parents have been taught that gay people are sick, despicable, trivial and dangerous, that homosexuality is one of the most shameful conditions known to man. Many parents cannot handle the guilt, shame and fear when they realize that their child is one of "them." The function of antilocutions is to instill these fears.

Antilocutions lead logically to the next stage in the acting out of prejudice, discrimination. If one believes a group is dangerous and sick, it is only natural that one must quarantine that group to keep it separate from those who are fearful.

Discrimination against gay people takes many forms. Space does not permit a lengthy discussion, but here are just a few examples. There are laws that say gay people may not enter the United States from abroad. Gay people are still fired from government jobs and discharged from the military solely because of their homosexuality. Teachers, physicians, and other professionals still run the risk of losing their professional rights if it is discovered that they are lesbian or gay. Parents can, and do, lose custody of their children because they are gay. Even in a liberal city like New York, gay couples can be thrown out of their apartments, with no recourse to law. In many states, wills have been overturned when a homosexual relationship is involved.[15]

Economic and legal discrimination are not the worst that can happen to minority groups. More devastating are those acts of social discrimination that corrode one's sense of self. For blacks, the signs that said they could drink only from water fountains set aside for their use, or must use separate toilets, were daily reminders that they were considered inferior, even in the basic human acts of alleviating thirst and of eliminating waste products. It is important to note that the incident that triggered the black civil rights movement of the fifties and sixties was not a lynching or an act of economic discrimination, but a matter involving humiliation and self-respect. In 1955, when that one woman, Rosa Parks, refused to move to the back of the bus in Montgomery Alabama she was responding to a need for self-respect. It is the denial of that need that causes the most damage to individual members of minority groups.

Although gay people are not forced to use separate toilets or water fountains (although the military does make the shared use of bathrooms an excuse for keeping gay people out of the military), they often suffer from equally corrosive denials of their humanity. The following example involves two lesbian lovers, one black, the other white. The black lesbian had to have surgery. Even though she had put her lover's name down as the one who was to receive all information and sign all papers (in other words, to act as what is usually called the next of kin), the surgeon refused to give her lover any information, on the grounds that she was not "family." Finally, in desperation, the lover told him, "She's my sister!" When she saw the disbelieving look on the physician's face, she said haughtily, "Different fathers."

The point is that, even on so basic a level as finding out the results of an operation on her lover, she had to resort to subterfuge. That is corrosive to one's self-respect.

Discrimination, coupled with antilocutions, leads inexorably to the next stage, violence. Violence against gay people is on the increase. This is, in part, a reaction to the gay liberation movement. Just as violence against blacks increased during the civil rights activities of the sixties, so too, gay and lesbian people are attacked because they are no longer willing to accept their assigned inferior status. In New York City alone, there are five physical attacks every two days against people suspected of being gay.

These acts of violence even include rape. Cities like New York, Chicago, and San Francisco have had to set up special rape centers for men who, thought to be gay, are attacked sexually. Lesbians are not exempt from this violence. There are many instances of lesbians who have been attacked on the streets and beaten so badly that they required hospitalization and long-term treatment.

This leads to a fourth stage in the process of prejudice, which is not described by Allport: the stage of oppression. "Oppression," a much abused and misused term, is used here to refer to the effects of the previous three stages of prejudice, and to the role prejudice plays as a maintaining factor in the stigmatization process.

One can easily see how lynchings were the direct outgrowth of antilocutions and discrimination. The person killed also served as a message to all other blacks and to the white society in which it occurred.

In like manner, gay people — especially gay and lesbian adolescents — are given the message that it is dangerous to be homosexually oriented. This message can be direct. I remember my own childhood in a lower-class Irish neighborhood in Philadelphia, when young men talked openly about rolling queers. No one seemed to think anything much of it. Those few who might have disagreed kept quiet. This is not now an irrelevant memory of a long-ago time. Recently, in Washington, D.C., several young men tortured and killed a congressman's aide, then went back to their neighborhood tavern and bragged about getting the queer. No one reported them.[16]

The message comes not only from violent low-lifes; respectable institutions within society cooperate. Many readers will probably have read of the man who went wild in Greenwich Village, killing and wounding several gay men with automatic weapon fire. One would think that such violence in one of the world's largest cities would receive extensive coverage by a newspaper like the *New York Times,* especially since it had, quite rightly, given front-page coverage to a similar action against a synagogue in Paris. But minimal coverage was given to the shootings. Indeed, more space was devoted in the same issue to "Who killed J.R.?" The message is clear. The shooting of a fictitious television character is more important than the killing of a bunch of faggots.

Again, the importance for this discussion lies in the effect the stages of prejudice have on gay and lesbian adolescents. The antilocutions, the discrimination, the violence and the oppression are the totality of a stigmatization process that creates special problems for gay and lesbian adolescents and makes them different.

Effects of Stigmatization

A great deal of research has documented the effects of stigmatization on blacks and Jews.[17] Very little has been done on the effects of stigmatization on gay people. This is surprising, since as early as the nineteenth century, researchers like Kraft-Ebing, Iwan Bloch and even Freud pointed out that many of the problems of the homosexually oriented were caused by societal oppression rather than by homosexuality itself.

As mentioned before, these difficulties are often associated with minority group membership of any kind, and while space does not permit an extensive discussion of these problems, some that are very relevant to any discussion of issues in delivery of services to gay and lesbian youth are:

1. denial of membership,
2. withdrawal and passivity,
3. identification with the dominant group; self-hate,
4. aggression against one's own group,
5. self-fulfilling negativism. (Allport, 1958)

All of these are interrelated, and each stems from the process I have already described. In a society in which even a father can say that the worst possible thing that could happen to his child is homosexuality, it is not too surprising that, as a young person slowly begins to realize that he or she is one of "them," that young person would develop these symptoms. Denial of membership becomes an almost inevitable result (Martin, 1982). Troiden documented this process in his work on the development of a healthy sexual identity in gay men (Troiden, 1979). He found that all his subjects went through a phase that he called "dissociation and signification." During this stage, the men recognized certain actions and feelings as homosexual, but denied their significance. Thus, overt homosexual acts became "a phase," "something I would grow out of," "just because there weren't any girls around" and so forth. These respondents had tried to separate themselves from the meaning of their acts, especially as they related to their possible membership in the hated group — homosexuals. These rationalizations and denials of group membership are often reinforced by well-meaning counsellors and therapists to the detriment of the individual gay person.

Denial of group membership is intimately entwined with identification with the dominant group and thus, self-hatred. If one believes that heterosexuality is indeed better than homosexuality, then one may often try to become heterosexual. The resulting failure can cause one to hate the homosexual desires that prevent complete identification with the dominant group. (This self-hatred now has an official name, courtesy of the American Psychiatric Association. Until 1987 it was called Ego Dystonic Homosexuality. It is now classified as a Sexual Disorder Not Otherwise Classified.) Self-hatred, in turn, can lead to aggression against one's own group. There are several tragic examples in recent cases involving public figures. One congressman, married and with children, was arrested for buying the services of teenage hustlers. He denied that he was homosexual. This same man was one of the most vociferous supporters of anti-gay legislation in Congress. Another congressman, discovered in homosexual activity, denied he was gay and got married to prove he was not. He was later arrested for committing homosexual sex acts in public. The leader of a leading conservative political action committee, which has sent anti-gay literature all over the country, was also recently revealed to be a homosexual.

For members of minority groups, their status can become an obsession characterized by what Allport called a "self-fulfilling negativism." Anything negative in one's life is seen as being caused by one's group membership. We have all heard the joke, applied to many different groups, about the severe stutterer who believed he did not get the job as a radio announcer because "they hate Jews," or blacks or Hispanics or whatever. Self-fulfilling negativism creates the attitude that one's own efforts mean nothing, that one's race, religion, sexual orientation or ethnic identity is an insurmountable barrier to achievement. The major problem is that there is often a grain of truth in the fear. But once an individual gives in completely to the belief, it becomes self-fulfilling. Sometimes young gay people will not seek out the help they are entitled to because they believe that they will be humiliated or treated badly. Many times, this is not the case; they would be treated with professional care and respect. But the strength of the fear negates the professionalism of those dedicated to helping them.

Throughout this paper, the emphasis has been that gay and lesbian adolescents are members of a minority group that is victim to a stigmatization process similar to that suffered by other hated groups. Some argue that this is not true. Unlike blacks or women, gay people can hide; therefore, they choose the problems they have. The ability to hide or not has nothing to do with the definition of minority status. No one would say that a Jew in an antisemitic society is not the victim of unjustified negative acts just because the Jew could pretend to be a Christian. Similarly, a Catholic in Northern Ireland or a light-skinned black in the United States would not be considered ineligible to be members of a minority group just because they could pass as members of the majority. Indeed, the very need to pass can be argued to be proof of the prejudice.

Nevertheless, while the ability to hide may have nothing to do with whether or not gay people are a minority, the possibility of hiding creates special problems that again serve to make gay and lesbian adolescents different from their heterosexual counterparts. Some of these issues are examined in depth in another paper and therefore will not be discussed extensively here (Martin, 1982). However, certain key issues will be touched upon.

The Greek word "stigma" originally referred to a visible sign. It could be a brand, a ritual scarring, or a form of enforced dress. In modern times, a stigma can either be visible or not. In a racist society, the colour of one's skin becomes the visible stigma. One's religion or sexual orientation, however, may also be a stigma and yet not be immediately visible. Goffman points out that this divides the stigmatized into two groups, the discredited and the discreditable (Goffman, 1963). Those who are discredited are those whose stigma is known or visible; those that are discreditable are those whose stigma is not visible or known, but for whom discovery will be disastrous. A person with a black skin, a Jew who must wear a Star of David, or a gay person forced to wear a pink triangle is discredited; those who can pass are discreditable.

Gay and lesbian adolescents can fall into either category. The young gay male who is discredited, either because he is "effeminate"[18] or because he has been discovered, faces reactions ranging from public humiliation to violence (Goffman, 1963). The youngster can handle this mistreatment in several ways, including the withdrawal and passivity noted above. For example, he can become truant or refuse to seek services or help. One major youth agency in New York has a reputation as being anti-gay.

Whether it is or not is irrelevant, since the gay kids on the street believe it is. The word is out that if you are known for being gay, you face trouble from both staff and the other kids being served. Therefore, for the most part, the gay kids who go to this agency are those who believe they can pass.

Sometimes a discredited youngster will handle anti-gay treatment by exaggerating the stigmatized behavior and fulfilling the expectations he or she believes that others have. Exaggerated mannerisms, cross-dressing, inappropriate sexual acting out, all can serve as a mechanism for coping as well as an expression of hostility.

The discredited gay youngster can raise havoc in an agency. Sometimes the disturbance comes from the kind of behavior just described. Cross-dressing can bring about a host of reactions, not only from staff but also from the other youths being served. However the turmoil is sometimes caused by staff reactions rather than by any kind of acting out by the youngster.

Recently, the Institute in New York was asked to help a settlement house in one of the outer boroughs. It had as a client a young black male who was very "obvious." His inability to hide had led to repeated physical and verbal attacks at school, so he became truant. The problem was not in the boy himself: he was quite happy at the settlement house and responding well to their various programs. The real difficulty lay in the battles that his presence was causing among the staff. Some wanted to treat him by making him more like a "real boy." They were insisting that he be forced to take part in the boxing and other sports programs offered by the agency. Others wanted to let him develop his own interests and perform in those areas where he felt most confident. For example, he had set up a very successful fashion show for the agency. The first group felt that this was feeding his "effeminacy" and that the second group was doing him a disservice; the second group argued that the others were bigoted and were continuing the kind of pressure that had made the young man become a truant in the first place. The resulting bad feeling was a disruptive force among the staff and had the potential to interfere with their other activities. To their credit, they sought help and advice. There are other documented situations in which a youngster has been made a scapegoat and, eventually, denied services.

Gay or lesbian adolescents who are discreditable face additional problems, most of which stem from their need to hide. At some level they know all the things that happen to discredited youngsters can happen to them as well. Therefore, they hide to avoid humiliations, expulsion from the family, even the possibility of violence. Unfortunately, often the effects of hiding are eventually even more devastating than the direct actions taken against those who are discovered. Hiding immediately poisons each and every relationship in which it is an issue. Homosexual adolescents must lie to their parents, siblings, friends and teachers. If they do not lie, the results can be disastrous. Many of these issues are discussed in the author's paper, "Learning To Hide: The Socialization of the Gay Adolescent" (Martin, 1982) and will not be reviewed here. The following quote sums up the problems faced by those who feel they must hide:

> The awareness of inferiority means that one is unable to keep out of consciousness the formulation of some chronic feeling of the worst sort of insecurity, and this means that one suffers anxiety and perhaps even something worse ... the fear that others can disrespect a person because of something he shows, means that he is always insecure in his contact with other people; ... now that represents an almost fatal deficiency of the self system.

Summary

As stated at the beginning of this chapter, the purpose was to try and provide a contextual framework within which to look at the problems and issues in the delivery of services to gay and lesbian youth. The context, basically, for gay and lesbian youth is that of victims caught in a society-wide process of stigmatization that, for them, has negative social, economic, and emotional effects. Within this process, young homosexuals either become discredited or discreditable, and each state creates special conditions and problems, not only for the young people themselves but also for those who must interact with them. Implicit within this framework is the notion that the youngsters' problems do not stem from their sexual orientation *per se*, but from the hatred that is directed toward them because of their sexual orientation. Unfortunately, their problems are often intensified because they have internalized this hatred.

It is clear that the deliverers of services to this population do not have an easy job. This book has been written in the hope that it will help professionals in their work with lesbian and gay youth.

PART II

Counselling Strategies and Issues

The first section of this book provided helping professionals with a framework in which to address the counselling and service needs of gay and lesbian youth. Included in it were general information about homosexuality, an examination of attitudes and beliefs, and a consideration of the meaning of being gay or lesbian. Also illustrated were some of the unique issues and conflicts confronting young gay and lesbian people, and a caution that a focus on sexual orientation must not obscure all the other characteristics which make these adolescents individuals. In the following chapters, some of the ways in which sexual orientation may become an issue when counselling lesbian and gay youth are examined; included are strategies for setting priorities, addressing the issues, and discussing specific topics including self-disclosure, confusion, and distress about being homosexual. The section concludes with a discussion of the counselling context.

CHAPTER 8

The Homosexual Adolescent in Need of Social Services

Not all gay or lesbian adolescents seek counselling or come to the attention of social services. Those who do so fall into two general categories. There are those who require counselling specifically because they are lesbian or gay; for example, they are isolated, in conflict with their parents because of their sexual orientation, or they are afraid of being homosexual. Others become involved with social services for the same reasons that their heterosexual counterparts do: they have broken the law; they are abused; they are drop-outs, runaways, unwed parents or drug abusers. Although the stress of being lesbian or gay can exacerbate existing problems, homosexuality itself, is not the reason that the latter group requires social services.

In this chapter several examples are used to illustrate how sexual orientation can emerge as a counselling issue. A strategy for establishing the client's priority of needs and assessing the relevance of sexual orientation issues is suggested.

Setting Priorities with Lesbian and Gay Clients

There is a two-step strategy for establishing the priority of needs of gay or lesbian clients and assessing the relevance of their sexual orientation. The first step is to set aside homosexuality temporarily and examine the remaining factors. This is accomplished most easily by putting the situation into a "heterosexual context." The following example illustrates this process.

In a recent workshop, a group of guidance counsellors described a situation at a local high school which was becoming problematic. They were concerned about a gay male student who was making indiscriminate advances toward other males in the school. The teachers were hesitant to become involved at all. Some were not sure the homosexual behavior was any of their business. Others worried that criticizing the student's behavior would be tantamount to censuring his sexual orientation. Yet they feared the student would be beaten up if they did not intervene. The teachers were asked whether they would intervene if the student were coming on to female students in the same manner. The answer was, "Yes, they would." When asked how they would intervene, the teachers proposed a number of alternatives, and were able to recognize that these options were also appropriate for dealing with the young gay man.

With the best of intentions, these teachers had been paralyzed by a combination of unspoken and erroneous assumptions: (a) that the problem was homosexual behavior; and, as a corollary (b) that the problem was outside of the realm of their expertise and responsibility. Temporarily altering the context in which they examined his behavior enabled them to switch their focus and to view the problem more constructively as a question of inappropriate behavior. Once this was established the teachers recognized the situation as something that not only could they address, but should address.

The second step is to put the homosexuality back into the picture to see how it modifies the situation if, in fact, it does. The young man in the example above might have been coming on to other boys because he was socially isolated from any gay peers and knew of no other way to deal with his isolation. If this were the case then helping him meet gay peers and role models might reduce his need to make contacts in inappropriate ways.

All adolescents need peers and role models, and service providers regularly help youth with both their peer relations and finding role models. When gay or lesbian adolescents need peers and role models, it is no different. A homosexual orientation changes the context, but not necessarily the service response, itself.

A complex example of the value of the two-step strategy involves a youngster who had a long-term involvement with social services. Mike was an impulsive, immature sixteen-year-old of dull-average intelligence. He had come to the attention of the Children's Aid Society because of truancy, running away from home and the parents' inability to control his comings and goings. When he ran away, he would take off for downtown Toronto and make some money by hustling. Mike's stated goal in life was to stay downtown, hustle, and live in an abandoned car. On two occasions he had sexually molested young boys, although none of the workers recently involved with Mike were aware of exactly what the circumstances had been. His erotic interest in children remained a concern, and he was eventually placed in secure-care treatment.

With varying degrees of certainty, Mike described himself as gay. In response, he was assigned a gay contract-worker, who spent several hours a week with him in the hope that an appropriate gay role model would be of some value. On an outing one day, Mike was left unsupervised, briefly, and ran away. When he came back, three months later, the agency placed him in a foster home with two gay men, who had no previous experience as foster parents. He ran away two days later. When Mike was apprehended he admitted to several instances of sexually molesting boys while he was on the run. At the time of this writing he was awaiting trial. He did not understand why his behavior was a problem and was relatively unconcerned about his future.

Mike was clearly a hard-to-serve client. Although the service plan developed for him addressed a comprehensive range of issues, the actual response to his deficits in the areas of social skills, ability to form friendships and occupational skills often took a back seat to his sexual orientation. On the unexamined assumption that he was gay, he was expected to interact with the gay community at a level of functioning far higher than his capabilities in the rest of his life. He was asked to make decisions about his sexual and affectional preference with little understanding of human relationships (indeed, his emotional immaturity was a contributing factor in his interest in children). He was expected to relate to foster parents whose only qualifications were good intentions and their sexual orientation. Had the sexual orientation issue been lifted out it would have become clear that Mike had to become a functioning person before he could determine whether or not he actually was gay, and, if so, become a functioning gay person.

Working with gay male prostitutes provides another example of the difficulty in distinguishing between the issue of sexual orientation and other life issues. These young men are often the products of broken homes and abuse. Runaways, frequently homeless, are usually unemployed with few, if any, job skills and often have been through multiple placements. They live a hand-to-mouth existence, reflecting an inability and unwillingness to plan for the future (Schneider & Tremble, 1985a). Life on the street is likely to have eroded what self-esteem they may have had.

Some young hustlers are straight. Some are gay. Some who claim to be straight are in conflict or confused about their sexual orientation. Gay, straight, in conflict or confused, these youngsters need the basics — adequate food, shelter and medical care. They may also need life-skill and job-skill training. Many need someone to talk to and someone to help them negotiate the complications of welfare benefits, medical insurance and other assistance programs. These young men hit the streets because they believe they have no place else to go. They stay on the streets for the camaraderie, the promises of easy money, the drugs, the excitement, and, of course, because they see no alternative.

The male prostitutes who are gay, in contrast to their male heterosexual counterparts, have unique ties to the street. For some of them, prostitution is more than a way of making money. It may be a way of avoiding conflicts about sexual orientation ("I'm not gay — I only do it for the money"). It may be perceived as a way of socializing, making contacts with other gay males and finding a meaningful relationship. Some hope that a well-to-do trick will take them home for a long-term arrangement. Some gay hustlers simply believe that being gay means either standing on street corners selling sex, or driving around the block looking for sex. Gay street kids often perceive gay life to be limited to bars, bathhouses and exploitative relationships. They have little knowledge of other facets of the gay community. They think they have no future because they are gay. Hence there is little motivation to get off the street.

Helping youth get off the street means assisting them to develop life-skills and job-skills, self-esteem, and a legitimate means of supporting themselves. For those who are gay it also involves examining and helping them recognize their limited conceptions about the "gay lifestyle" and the gay community, exploring with them their options for socializing within the community, and addressing their conflicts about being gay. In summary, being gay does not put these young men on the street. However, issues regarding sexual orientation are among those that need to be addressed before these young men will be capable of getting themselves off the street.

These three examples illustrate the varying degrees and ways in which sexual orientation can be an issue; they also illustrate the appropriate steps for assessing the importance of sexual orientation relative to the other issues.

Once it is established that sexual orientation is an issue that needs to be addressed, there are a number of inquiries to be made by the worker.

The first inquiry is to find out how the adolescent feels about being gay or lesbian and what the meaning of being gay or lesbian is for the adolescent. Does the young, gay runaway have a distorted image of the "gay lifestyle," based on his experience on the street? Does the male who dresses in women's clothes, a transvestite, believe that this is the only way that gay men dress? Does the suicidal young lesbian believe that she will never enjoy a long-term, stable, intimate relationship?

The second query is to discover if the adolescent attributes all his/her difficulties to being homosexual. The realities of discrimination and hostility toward homosexuals cannot be discounted or ignored; however, the youngster who claims to have no friends because he is gay often has poor social skills. Likewise, an adolescent who claims she cannot get work because she is a lesbian may have no marketable job skills. Like their heterosexual counterparts who are jobless or friendless, these adolescents might need life-skills and job training. They may also need some reality testing — Can most people really guess that they are gay? Do most people actually care if they are gay?

The third question is a delicate one, and it is to determine if the adolescent is using sexual orientation as a way of victimizing him/herself; frequently, adolescents in need of service are self-destructive. They act out, want attention, and will go to extremes to get it. They know how to use their sexuality — homosexual or heterosexual — to shock or embarrass. They know that acting out the stereotype of the gay male or lesbian may invite abuse, derision or violence from their peers but they do so anyway. This is not to suggest that homosexuals are to blame for their own victimization, however, some youngsters use their sexuality to their own detriment, and homosexual adolescents are no exception.

When a young gay or lesbian client behaves in a provocative way, workers can ask themselves and their client these questions: Is the client deliberately victimizing him/herself? If so, what are the likely consequences of this behavior? Does the client understand the consequences, and is s/he prepared for them? What is the client trying to communicate to others or trying to get them to do? Apply the *same* criteria that you would in evaluating provocative behavior from any clients. While it is often desirable to allow adolescents to act out and learn from the consequences of their behavior, if they are in real danger, they need protection. The worker's reaction depends upon the youth, the client-worker relationship and the severity of the consequences.

The above section contains suggestions for strategies to be used in evaluating the relevance of sexual orientation, and for establishing and ordering the issues when a client is lesbian or gay. Each of the next three sections discuss situations in which sexual orientation becomes the main focus of attention.

CHAPTER 9

"I Don't Want to be Gay"

Conceptualizing the Issues

In a world where homosexuality is considered by most people to be a crime, a sin, or an illness it is not surprising that some adolescents are deeply distressed at being lesbian or gay, stating categorically that they do not want to be homosexual. This distress may be interpreted as part of the coming-out process or as a mental illness, as explained below.

1. **A stage in the coming-out process.** Most gay males and lesbians feel distressed at the thought of being homosexual at some time during the coming-out process. Most models and descriptions of the coming-out process (eg. Cass, 1979; Coleman, 1982; Cronin, 1974) include a phase of conflict during which the individual (a) denies or suppresses homosexual feelings, (b) rejects homosexuality and being identified as homosexual, and (c) often feels depressed, anxious, or self-destructive. Eventually individuals can, and usually do, with social support, come to accept their sexual orientation and ultimately find pleasure and fulfillment in same-sex relationships. The lesbian or gay male who says, "I'm gay and I don't want to be," can be thought of as going through a conflict phase.

2. **Interpretation as a mental illness.** Although homosexuality *per se* is no longer considered to be a mental illness, "persistent and marked distress about one's sexual orientation" (p. 296) is included as a "Sexual Disorder Not Otherwise Specified" in the revised *Diagnostic and Statistical Manual*, a

compendium of all the categories of mental illness as defined by the American Psychiatric Association (1987). (This replaces "Ego-Dystonic Homosexuality" which appeared in an earlier edition [American Psychiatric Association, 1983]). This term is used to describe a homosexual who wants to be heterosexual. Theoretically it could also describe a heterosexual who wants to be homosexual, but it is unlikely that it would be used in this way. Clearly this category refers to distressed homosexuals.

Each of the above perspectives suggests the need for a different therapeutic goal for the distressed client. If the distress is conceptualized as part of the coming-out process, then the goals of coming out, described in Chapter 6, become the objectives of the therapeutic process. That is to say, the goal is to develop gay-affirmative feelings. On the other hand, the interpretation which labels this distress as mental illness, while not ruling out gay-affirmative counselling, tends to endorse a change in sexual orientation as the goal.

In order to evaluate these disparate approaches, it is useful to examine the distress in its societal context. To do so, the analogy of minority racial groups living in a largely white society will be used.

Self-hatred, alienation, and distress are common among stigmatized minorities. As explained in Chapter 7, stigmatization can lead to a number of emotional problems related to identity — including denial of membership in the stigmatized group and identification with the attitudes of the dominant group. For example, light-skinned blacks who try to pass as white or non-black often internalize negative attitudes toward blacks. The result is self-hatred.

Black Rage, (Grier & Cobbs, 1968) written in the 1960s, documents the depression and anxiety of black clients in therapy who have internalized the stereotypical image of blacks. For these clients, therapy is a process of rejecting the negative stereotype and accepting themselves as black. Clearly, the real problem for these clients is not being black — instead, it is distress at being black in a white society which largely rejects minorities. Hiding or rejecting one's black identity is not the solution. Rather, it is rejoicing in being black, which was the underlying logic of the "Black is Beautiful" movement.

The problem with being black, Jewish, East Indian, or Asian is the arbitrary and unjust stigmatization by the dominant culture. Similarly, conflicts regarding sexual orientation are societally based. It would be inappropriate to label the distress inherent in being a member of a minority as mental illness. Likewise, it is inappropriate to label the distressed homosexual as mentally ill.

However, unlike other minority group members, homosexuals do not grow up in a supportive cultural milieu which acts as a buffer against stigmatization. When gay or lesbian adolescents are called "fags" or "lezzies,"

usually

they have no one at home to help them maintain self-esteem in the face of prejudice. This may be confounded by the fact that their cultural or religious backgrounds may condemn homosexuality. Gay and lesbian adolescents have no accurate information or role models from whom to learn how to manage issues arising from their sexuality. In a society which unquestioningly expects them to be heterosexual, gay and lesbian adolescents are unprepared for their emerging homosexual identity, and there is no readily available framework in which young homosexuals can come to understand and accept their sexual orientation (Hetrick & Martin, 1983). It is no wonder that young people are often distressed when they realize they are lesbian or gay.

Conceptualizing the adolescent's distress at being homosexual as an outcome of stigmatization has some implications for a therapeutic response. These are discussed below.

Implications for a Therapeutic Approach

Service providers may wonder whether or not clients in conflict over their sexual orientation should be helped or encouraged to "go straight," especially when clients, themselves, identify their sexual feelings as the source of the problem, having failed to recognize stigmatization as a contributing factor. "After all," they might reason, "wouldn't life be easier as a heterosexual?" There are a number of responses to this, all of which suggest that going straight is not the preferred therapeutic goal.

Encouraging clients to change their sexual orientation is to encourage them to deny or repress an essential part of themselves, thereby conveying the message that there is, indeed, something essentially wrong with homosexuality. Therapy which leads to denial, repression, and self-hatred is hardly commendable. According to a research review conducted by Ronald Langevin (1984), a psychologist at the Clarke Institute of Psychiatry in Toronto, even if change were an appropriate therapeutic goal, evidence indicates that sexual orientation cannot be changed. In reaching this conclusion, Langevin distinguishes between sexual feelings and sexual behavior. Most people can and do respond sexually, with varying degrees of intensity, to a range of physical stimuli. Almost two-thirds of gay men and five-sixths of lesbians have had heterosexual physical relations (Bell & Weinberg, 1978; Kinsey, et al., 1948, 1953). Thus, very distressed clients may be motivated, willing and able to cease homosexual behavior in favor of exclusively heterosexual behavior. However, in most, if not all, cases, homoerotic feelings and the preference for same-sex relationships remain fixed. Homosexuals who appear to be "going straight" are usually settling for relationships which are second best for them, sexually and emotionally (see also, Martin [1984a]).

Trying to change the homosexual into a heterosexual has other conse-quences. The futility and frustration of unsuccessfully attempting to change adds fuel to clients' feelings of inadequacy and distress. It introduces greater developmental lag, misdirecting youngsters from the tasks involved in the coming-out process. Therapy directed toward changing sexual orientation, successful or not, implies that homosexuality is sinful, criminal, or sick, and further feeds self-hatred and despair (Davison, 1977). Individuals who continue to experience homoerotic feelings, even after overt sexual behavior has been modified, will be rejecting that part of themselves, expending valuable psychological energy suppressing and denying those feelings throughout life. Thus, even if behavior were modified, individuals would still be left with the task of coming to terms with their homoerotic feelings.

In summary, helping the client develop a gay-affirmative outlook is the most appropriate therapeutic response. How to do this will be discussed next.

Responding to the client

There are a number of questions which need to be answered in order to facilitate the development of gay-affirmative feelings.

1. *Level of information.* How much accurate information does the youngster have about homosexuality, and to what extent has the youngster internalized the myths and stereotypes? What does it mean to the adolescent to be gay or lesbian?

2. *External pressure.* Who or what are the influences which are motivating the adolescent to change — parents, peers, religious teachings or cultural background? Identifying these may suggest ways to reduce the pressure.

3. *Other issues.* Gay and lesbian adolescents usually find their way into the social service stream because of issues other than their sexual orientation. These issues are often of more immediate concern to the client. In those instances where sexual orientation is the major issue, usually there will be a number of related problems — conflict with parents regarding sexual orientation, poor school performance as a result of depression or anxiety, suicidal ideation (or actual attempts), to name a few. All the issues involved need to be identified and priorities need to be set. Focussing the majority of time and attention on the youth's sexuality, when the youngster has no place to live, is failing in school or has a deficit of social skills may not be sensible. It may be preferable to address the issue of sexual orientation after more immediate problems are resolved.

4. *Perceived consequences of being heterosexual.* How does the youngster perceive that life will change if s/he is heterosexual? It is easy to attribute all negative reactions to one's minority status. ("I can't get a job because I'm black," "No one likes me because I'm an undertaker." "They don't give me good grades because I'm gay.") The lesbian or gay youngster who makes this attribution will need to examine the assumption that the key to success is to be heterosexual. In addition, what does the adolescent believe the future will be like as a homosexual? Does the youth imagine that he or she will have to live out the stereotype of a gay man or lesbian?

5. *Access to role models.* Has the adolescent met any other gays or lesbians? As discussed in Chapter 6, meeting lesbian and gay peers is often a turning point in the coming-out process as youngsters see for themselves that homosexuality will not destroy their lives. However, distressed adolescents may be too afraid or ashamed of their homosexuality to want any contact with other homosexuals. Workers may be able to devise non-threatening ways to help adolescents make that first contact.

Conflicts over sexual orientation are painful, distressing and may be persistent. However, with time, support and work in other areas of conflict, the issue can be resolved as the therapeutic problem is transformed from "Can I be heterosexual?" to "How can I accept my homosexual feelings?"

If an adolescent persists in wanting to be heterosexual, the worker has some decisions to make, and may find that none of the options seem to be entirely satisfactory. The worker may decide that this is not a process s/he cares to be part of and may choose to refer the client to someone else. Alternatively, the worker may decide to support the client in the decision to go straight and help search for a therapist. Trying to go straight may be a painful but necessary part of the coming-out process for that youngster, who ultimately may decide to try and accept a lesbian or gay identity.

CHAPTER 10

Gay or Straight?:
The Confused Adolescent

In the best of all possible worlds, young people reach adolescence with a sense of trust in the world around them, a developing sense of self-regulation and independence, and an excitement about exploring life. They face a variety of developmental tasks as a growing awareness of sexuality emerges, often marked by an approach-avoidance conflict about actual sexual experimentation. It is within this context, that the adolescent is asking, "Who am I?" The pathway to answering this question is fraught with confusion for most young people.

During this period of development, youngsters have an opportunity to try out different social roles. Within limits, young people are offered a chance for social experimentation without much consequence or penalty. For example, most adults are prepared to live with the adolescent who dresses outrageously in order to be part of the youth culture. The behavior is tolerated in the belief that young people can benefit from the opportunity to make their own decisions and live with the consequences, at a time in their lives when they are not required to make life-long commitments to lifestyles or preferences. Most teenagers do not remain on the fringe. Their experimentation usually leads them back to an acceptance of the values with which they were raised. Amidst this general adolescent confusion and experimentation, some youngsters may be struggling with the question of sexual orientation as well. How does this issue arise?

Throughout adolescent development, sexual awareness emerges, the capacity for close friendships develops, older role models become mentors and idols, and adolescents begin to be aware of a variety of attractions. They may occasionally feel a physical attraction to the same sex. Most experiment sexually, and some, in a variety of circumstances, will have homosexual experiences. Some of these adolescents will think that they are lesbian or gay. Some will be confused by their feelings or experiences. The specific cause of the confusion may be different for those who ultimately decide that they are homosexual and those who ultimately decide that they are heterosexual.

Before the worker can help young people determine their sexual orientation, it is necessary to understand the range of factors which can contribute to confusion both for adolescents who ultimately will be homosexual and for those adolescents who ultimately will be heterosexual. In the following section, confusion as experienced by each of these two groups will be considered separately.

Confusion in the Straight Adolescent *(Good)*

Becoming a sexual person is difficult for most adolescents. It often brings young people into conflict with their family and church. These conflicts are compounded by factors including the fear of disease, the need for acceptance from peers and lack of emotional maturity. The object of one's sexual attractions may become problematic if that person is someone from a different race or religion, or if the attraction is for someone of the same sex.

Within this context of conflict, most adolescents make judgments about their sexuality and sexual orientation not only with a paucity of accurate information but also with an abundance of misinformation which includes myths and contemporary images of sexual intimacy. The following exemplifies the ways in which these factors contribute to confusion.

1. **Inaccurate information.** Lack of accurate information can lead adolescents as well as adults to reach erroneous conclusions about many aspects of their sexuality. Sexual orientation is no exception. A common mistake is the failure to distinguish homosexual behavior from a truly homosexual sexual orientation. It is erroneously believed that occasional homosexual fantasies, feelings, or experiences mean that an individual is a homosexual. On the contrary, as explained in Chapter 1, many heterosexuals have had homosexual experiences and feelings. These, in themselves, do not necessarily mean that the individual is lesbian or gay. In a similar vein, a lack of interest in heterosexual sex is sometimes erroneously interpreted as a sign of homosexuality rather than a mere lack of sexual interest. As a consequence of these erroneous beliefs, heterosexual adolescents who have had

some homosexual experiences jump to the conclusion that they are indeed gay or lesbian. Adolescents who are hesitant and shy about sex amidst increasing peer pressure to experiment sexually, may wonder whether they are gay or lesbian, especially when peers seem to be enjoying frequent sexual activity.

2. **Unrealistic expectations.** Portrayals of sexual activity in the media, as well as the bravado of peers, lead adolescents to have unrealistic expectations about the sex act. Young people may believe that they should be responsive whenever a sexual opportunity arises, and may expect that sex will be consistently pleasurable. They often fail to understand the range of responses, interest, and readiness which individuals experience. The consequences of this are illustrated by the example of a fifteen-year-old who had sexual intercourse with her boyfriend for the first time without using birth control, after watching a pornographic movie. The experience was a disaster, as was a second attempt some weeks later. On the basis of this limited experience, the young woman decided that she must be a lesbian, since heterosexual sex had been so disappointing.

3. **Myths and stereotypes.** Young people who erroneously subscribe to the stereotype of masculine lesbians and effeminate gay males may wonder whether they themselves are homosexual if they do not fit traditional gender roles. For example, a young man who does not have traditional male interests, such as contact sports, may wonder if he is gay, especially if he is derided by his peers calling him "faggot" or "queer," common terms of derision among adolescents. He may take these labels to heart, not only misapprehending what it means to be homosexual, but also being unclear about the meaning of being masculine and heterosexual. Another example, is the young man, socialized as a male to hide his emotions, who might wonder if he is gay when he simply feels affection for his same-sex friends.

Young women may be less vulnerable to the pitfalls of myths and stereotypes about homosexuality since North American culture is tolerant, up to a point, of tomboys; besides, demonstrations of same-sex affection are also more common and acceptable among females than males. Nonetheless, girls may also experience confusion if they do not adopt traditional feminine gender roles.

The roots of confusion for youths who are essentially heterosexual will vary from individual to individual; however, these three areas seem to have the greatest potential for creating confusion among adolescents who are essentially heterosexual.

Confusion for Lesbian and Gay Adolescents

The myths and stereotypes of homosexuality and heterosexuality play a major role in the confusion experienced by lesbian and gay adolescents. Equally important is the fact that emerging homosexual feelings are both unexpected and unwelcome to most adolescents. This combination of factors can create confusion in the following ways.

1. **Myths and stereotypes.** Adolescents who ultimately decide that they are lesbian or gay are just as likely as anyone else to endorse the erroneous stereotypes of homosexuals. An athletic young man who is experiencing same-sex sexual attractions may say to himself, "All gay men are effeminate so I can't be gay." Similarly, an attractive, feminine young woman may deny the possibility that she is a lesbian since she does not want to dress like a man. Thus, young people may fail to recognize or acknowledge homosexual feelings because they do not fit the stereotype.

2. **Inability to label feelings.** "Falling in love," or feeling "sexually aroused" are terms which are usually used in a heterosexual context. Initially, they do not seem to translate easily to describe feelings for people of the same sex. Consequently, homosexual feelings can be difficult to identify and articulate. Without a vocabulary to express homosexual feelings, a youngster often believes no one else in the world feels that way.

3. **Dismissal of feelings.** Adults who trivialize or dismiss adolescents' homosexual feelings as "just a crush" or "a phase" contribute to the confusion. As one young man commented,

> My mother told me that it was just a phase that many boys went through, and not to worry. So I didn't. When the phase lasted three or four years, I started to think to myself, "Gee, this is a long phase."

4. **Conflicts about homosexuality.** Understandably, most homosexuals go through a period of not wanting to be gay or lesbian. The fear of rejection and stigmatization is the basis for denying, rejecting and fighting against homosexual feelings. The conflict between the feelings and the fears results in confusion.

5. **Sexual abuse.** Mental health professionals, sensitized to the sexual abuse of children, often ask whether such experiences can make a youngster gay or lesbian. There is no evidence to suggest that sexual abuse of any sort can make a youngster gay or lesbian, although sexual abuse can create confusion.

Gay or lesbian youngsters who believe that abuse "made" them that way may reject their sexuality, perceiving it negatively as a symptom of the abuse. For example, in a recent conversation, a young lesbian who had been sexually abused described how she had resisted her homoerotic feelings because she believed they were emerging "for all the wrong reasons" — that they derived from a fear and rejection of males. During therapy she came to realize that her feelings about women had a legitimacy of their own rather than being merely an avoidance of men. The confusion was resolved as she became able to separate her feelings about men and sexual abuse from her feelings about women.

Sometimes, youngsters may become guilt-ridden as well as confused, if they experience some sexual arousal or pleasure during an abusive sexual experience. When this happens to young men who have been abused by adult males they may say, "I'm gay because I was abused," or "If he chose me as his victim, it must mean I'm gay," or "If I was aroused, I must be gay." To them this means they are gay due to a negative experience and being gay is therefore negative. As youngsters separate their reactions to sexual abuse from their present feelings about the same or the opposite sex, the confusion arising from these conflicts will begin to resolve itself.

Summary

There are many sources of confusion for gay, lesbian, and heterosexual adolescents. Workers attempting to assist an adolescent in resolving this confusion need an awareness of these factors. However, working effectively with a confused adolescent does not require that the outcome be predetermined or predictable. The process of working through the confusion is the same, regardless what the adolescent ultimately turns out to be — gay, lesbian or straight.

Working with a youth who is confused about sexual orientation is much like working with confusion concerning any issue. Confusion indicates that there are conflicts about (a) values, (b) interpreting the meanings of events, and (c) feelings. Confusion exists where there is a lack of accurate information. Finding the source of the conflict, facilitating the expression of feelings and providing adequate information will help dissipate the confusion.

Resolving the Confusion

Independent of any input from parents, teachers, or peers, some youngsters come to the conclusion that they are definitely gay or lesbian, even though some adults in their life may not share the adolescent's certainty about that decision. However, unless young people invite a discussion of the issue, little will be achieved through an intrusive examination of their sexuality. When adolescents disclose that they are gay or lesbian, the worker is certainly justified in asking how that decision was reached, but cannot assume permission to question that position. It may be necessary to wait patiently until the adolescent extends consent.

Some youngsters who are confused about their sexual orientation may be able to articulate that confusion and ask for help in reaching a resolution. Others are so paralyzed by their confusion that they are unable to verbalize the nature of their difficulty. However, they may demonstrate behaviorally that something is troubling them. The following behaviors are indications that a young person may be struggling with the issue of sexual orientation:

1. Clothing, mannerisms, or affectations may indicate that the youngster is attempting to conform to the stereotype of the gay man or lesbian. Stereotypical behavior may be used to convey a variety of messages but is certain to get some attention.

2. Heterosexual promiscuity may be a desperate attempt by the gay or lesbian adolescent to affirm a heterosexual orientation. For straight youth, it may serve to ward off fears that they might be homosexual.

3. An unusually strong interest in talking about sexuality, especially when questions or comments reflect considerable misunderstanding, certainly indicates general problems with sexuality.

4. References to the homosexual experiences of other people, real or fictitious, or to something that happened years ago may be the adolescent's way of testing the waters to determine whether the worker is a reliable, safe person in whom to confide.

5. Concerns may be raised by a third party, such as the youngster's parents or teachers. Typically, these are not concerns about overt sexual behavior. More often, they refer to an inexplicable, growing social distance. Parents no longer know who their youngster's friends are, or where they socialize. A teacher or guidance counsellor may sense that the youngster is drawing away from school, becoming less involved in school activities, friendships and academic achievement.

6. Disinterest in the opposite sex must be interpreted with caution. When an introverted and withdrawn youngster shows little interest in the opposite sex, inferences about sexual orientation are unwarranted. On the other hand, when outgoing and enthusiastic youngsters show a disinterest in the opposite sex which is inconsistent with the quality of their relationships with same sex peers, it suggests that sexual orientation may be an issue.

The key concept is struggle. None of these factors, either together or separately, say anything more about a youngster's sexuality than that the individual may be struggling with an issue of identity, possibly a sexual concern, and perhaps sexual orientation. These factors must be weighed in combination, and in the context of the worker's general knowledge about the adolescent. Furthermore, this list is not exhaustive. Adolescents will act out anxieties, conflicts and confusion in unique and various ways. It rests with the worker to recognize and interpret signs of distress.

When a youngster appears to be confused about sexuality and/or sexual orientation, the worker must first decide whether this issue is relevant to the work at hand. If, for example, the task is to help the adolescent get into a school program or find financial assistance, sexuality may not be a legitimate issue, even if it appears that the youngster could benefit from help in that area. It may, however, become a *relevant* issue if the adolescent introduces it, or if the conflict is interfering with the general level of functioning.

If sexual orientation appears to be a legitimate topic of discussion, it needs to be raised in a non-threatening way. A direct confrontation is risky, leading easily to suspicion, avoidance or denial. There are two contexts at least in which adolescents can approach the issue of sexuality with a feeling of safety. The first is a discussion of relationships and how relationships work for them, and how they perceive, experience and deal with intimacy. Such a discussion of human relationships can lead to a reflection of the worker's own feelings about relationships and the value of closeness, intimacy and acceptance. This may communicate to the youngster that the worker is an approachable, trustworthy person. As well, it creates a comfort zone, allowing adolescents to inject the topic of sexuality when it becomes appropriate and comfortable to do so.

Discussions of masculinity and femininity may also facilitate communication. Talking about the meaning of these terms to the adolescent, and what it means to be a man or a woman, will help disentangle the issue of sexual orientation from issues relating to gender role and personal presentation. In addition, it will help youngsters understand and articulate how they experience their own masculinity or femininity.

These topics, in and of themselves, are important for adolescents. Sexual orientation is more than sexual behavior. It also involves emotional attachments and raises issues concerning gender role. Helping individuals understand how they want to relate to people and how they want to demonstrate intimacy can be productive in helping them examine sexuality as one potential aspect of relating to others. Separating the issue of sexual orientation from that of gender role helps to clarify the confusion which originates from stereotypical images of homosexuality.

Confusion is part of adolescence. It can also be part of the coming-out process. Although confusion is uncomfortable to experience, it is not in itself the problem, and part of the adolescent's work may be to learn to live with it for a while. Neither the youth, nor the worker should feel pressed by the confusion to come to a premature, perhaps erroneous, conclusion about the youth's sexual orientation.

Many adolescents do not resolve the issue of sexual orientation until in young adulthood, when they are on their own at college or in the work force. The identity consolidation which takes place for young people at this age often brings clarity to a confused young adult. Therefore, workers may not witness the ultimate resolution of adolescent conflict. However, youngsters can be provided with a gay-affirmative feeling as well as skills in coping, decision-making, and communication, to put in the bank, so to speak, until they have matured sufficiently to re-examine issues related to sexual orientation. It is less important for youngsters who are anxious or confused to decide on sexual preference than it is for them to be in touch with their sexual and emotional feelings, to develop a sense of self-worth and learn life skills.

Dilemmas for the Worker

Because homosexuality is such a sensitive subject, workers encounter pitfalls they would not experience in other areas of counselling. This section deals with sources of confusion for the worker.

Resolving issues concerning sexual orientation is much like any decision-making process, and should be treated accordingly. Clients who experience confusion about any issue, such as deciding whether or not to move out on their own or leave school, may press their worker to tell them what to do. Empathizing with the client's discomfort, workers may feel obliged to provide an answer. This is particularly compelling when the decision concerns an emotionally charged issue such as sexual orientation; but, to do so would be ill advised.

Workers are not expected to decide for adolescents whether they are gay or straight, and it is not necessary to divine the answer before productive work can take place. Regardless of the source of the confusion, the process of unravelling it is the same — provide information and discern where the conflicts lie. This focus on process will shift the attention from the emotionally laden content which impedes sound counselling practice.

Recognizing the stigma attached to homosexuality, workers often wonder whether the confused adolescent ought to be encouraged to "go straight." Although this strategy might seem to be in the youth's best interests, it creates a number of problems. For the ultimately homosexual adolescent, this strategy can be destructive. Many of these adolescents attempt to go straight by dating and experimenting sexually. This often becomes an exercise in frustration, resulting in low self-esteem, generated by the failure to develop romantic and sexual interest in the opposite sex or to perform sexually. Encouraging a youth to go straight, or interpreting homosexual feelings or behavior as "just a phase," impedes development for the developing gay or lesbian adolescent. It serves to delay the coming-out process, and with it, the developmental tasks of adolescence.

Directing the ultimately straight adolescent toward heterosexuality, while not misleading, may interfere with an examination process which must be undertaken in order to put same-sex attractions or sexual behavior into perspective. Only through such an examination can the issue of sexual orientation be adequately addressed and resolved.

In short, a worker is rarely justified in encouraging a client to go in one direction or another. Neither the interests of the ultimately lesbian or gay youth, nor those of the ultimately straight adolescent are served by encouragement to go straight.

Summary

Confusion is a part of growing up. In that context, some adolescents will be confused about their sexual orientation. Although the source of confusion may be different for ultimately lesbian, gay or straight adolescents, the process of resolving confusion is the same. Youngsters will have to learn to cope during the process of identifying and resolving the conflicts until the confusion dissipates.

CHAPTER 11

Self Disclosure and the Family

During the initial stages of the coming-out process, whether or not to disclose one's sexual orientation to family, friends, and associates is one of the most pressing issues. It is a matter which will arise repeatedly throughout life but, for most people, the most difficult disclosure is telling their parents. This chapter is concerned with helping young people prepare to do this.

Reasons for Disclosure

Many people question why homosexuals have to make a point of revealing their sexual orientation to others. What homosexuals do in private is no more relevant than what heterosexuals do, yet heterosexuals do not feel compelled to confide or announce their heterosexuality. This is because there are some fundamental differences in the experiences of heterosexuals and homosexuals.

In a world in which everyone is assumed to be heterosexual (correctly most of the time), a declaration of one's sexual proclivities is generally deemed to be neither necessary nor in good taste. Based on the assumption of heterosexuality, a whole series of assumptions are made about a person's lifestyle and relationships. For example, when a man and woman live together it is usual to assume that their relationship is an intimate one — emotionally and physically. This assumption affects how family, friends, and acquaintances relate to the pair. For example, both are usually included in invitations to the parents' homes for holidays, and often share a bedroom if they stay overnight. When one partner is seriously ill and hospitalized, the other has certain visiting privileges as a recognized member of the immediate family. The heterosexual assumption, when correct, provides a framework for understanding, or beginning to understand, the nature of a relationship, allowing many things to be left unsaid.

Similarly, knowing when someone is gay or lesbian can provide a framework for understanding certain parts of his/her life. For example, understanding that "roommates" are lovers, one can appreciate their excitement at moving in together as well as their despair if they separate. One does not expect to be privy to intimate details, but can still share the same joys and sorrows, as with any close friend.

Self-disclosure allows gay men or lesbians to talk as freely as heterosexuals do about lovers and friends. They can also discuss activities which take place in the gay community. People who are not "out" to close friends and family often feel alienated, dishonest, and unreal. They must lie about where they have been if they have attended a meeting of a local lesbian and gay group. They humor parents who envision for their children a traditional future involving marriage and children of their own. They equivocate when the family doctor asks if they are sexually active and whether they need birth control. Parents of gay and lesbian youngsters often notice a growing sense of distance from their children, unaware that their youngster is establishing ties in the gay and lesbian community. With concern, they gradually realize that they no longer know where their child is going and who his/her friends are. For the youngster's part, the constraint of remaining closeted may manifest itself in irritation and frustration, and give rise to bickering over inconsequential matters. This drives the family apart even further.

Hiding such an integral part of one's identity can undermine psychological well-being. Findings of studies have associated a hidden gay or lesbian identity with feelings of depression and futility, physiological malfunctions such as ulcers and hypertension, low frustration thresholds, awkwardness in interpersonal relationships, shame, and anxiety (Bayley, 1974; Brooks, 1981 Dank, 1971; Weinberg & Williams, 1974). Nondisclosure also seems to block other areas of functioning, such as creativity (Lee, 1977). It is as if it is impossible to repress selectively only one facet of the self. Censoring information is an ongoing, stressful process.

> Every once in a while my lover slips and calls me "sweetie" in front of people who don't know we're lesbians. Everyone pretends they haven't noticed — but I don't know. We try hard, but we slip up sometimes. (lesbian, age 26)

Everyone at work noticed how tired I was, but I just couldn't get into explaining how I was up all night with my lover who had the stomach flu. I guess it might not have raised any eyebrows that a guy happened to stay at my house overnight, but I couldn't take the chance. (gay male, age 27)

and:

Someone in my class started talking about AIDS, and they really didn't know what they were talking about. But I felt like I had to keep quiet, because if I knew too much they might guess that I was gay. (gay male, age 17)

One of the greatest sources of stress is the fear that someone important will find out unexpectedly. When this happens, individuals have no time to prepare, cannot articulate the disclosure exactly the way they would wish to, and may be faced with a crisis with which they are not ready to cope. Furthermore, when parents or friends do inadvertently find out, they are frequently hurt or disappointed that they were not taken into confidence.

In addition to stress, the closeted homosexual is more likely than an uncloseted counterpart to have negative feelings about being gay (Lee, 1977; McDonald, 1982), however, the cause-and-effect relationship between negative feelings and being closeted is not straightforward. While the negative feelings may motivate the individual to remain closeted, studies suggest that self-disclosure actually contributes to gay-positive feelings and higher self-esteem (Brooks, 1981). Perhaps the exercise of working through the ramifications of disclosure and facing the consequences (which may not be as catastrophic as expected) contributes to increased gay-positive feelings.

Theorists contend that overall identity formation is hampered when one's sense of self is incongruent with one's public image (Josselson, 1980). The ultimate result of a rift between the real self and the public self can be neurosis and psychosis (Laing, 1965). While remaining closeted does not make people psychotic, many young people do refer to the "schizophrenic" nature of their lives:

I'd spend most afternoons after school at my lover's house. Often we'd make love, and then I would ride my bike home to Rosedale and have dinner with my family who had no idea that I'd rather have been with Barbara at that moment. I'd look around the dining room table and feel like screaming. (lesbian, age 17)

I spent most weekends with these women, most of whom were a lot older than me. I'd play hockey with them and go to the bars, even though I was only sixteen. Then I'd go back to school each Monday. What could I say when people talked about their weekends? I felt like I was two different people during the week and then on the weekend. (lesbian, age 24)

Self-disclosure also has social and political significance for the politically aware. It may be perceived as a necessary rite of passage in establishing a sense of identity as a lesbian or gay person and a place in the gay community. Some lesbians and gay men who do not fit the stereotype feel a responsibility to become visible in order to raise the consciousness of the public.

In summary, self-disclosure alleviates stress and its accompanying symptoms, promotes a sense of identity, and contributes to higher self-esteem.

Although disclosure can be beneficial in the long run, there are risks. Some people may never be able to accept a gay or lesbian colleague, friend, or family member. Parents in particular may have great difficulty accepting their homosexual son or daughter, and it is this disclosure which is usually the most anxiety-provoking for gays and lesbians. The next section will review the considerations which must be made before coming out to parents.

Coming Out to Parents: Deciding and Planning Ahead

Coming out to parents requires planning, and should not be done impulsively. A social worker, therapist or counsellor can play an important part in the decision-making and planning process.

Deciding whether or not to disclose involves: (a) weighing the risks and benefits, including parental response; and (b) examining the client's motivation.

Planning for the disclosure involves considering: (a) the message, (b) method, (c) timing, (d) parents' probable reaction, and (e) support. These factors are discussed below.

Decision Making

1. **Weighing the costs and benefits.** Although disclosure can be beneficial in the long run, coming out to parents can be an upsetting experience for all concerned. As already noted above, some parents may never accept a homosexual child. The potential costs of disclosure may outweigh the potential benefits in some instances.

The first step in deciding whether to disclose is to try to anticipate the parental response and to assess how likely they are to come to terms with their child's sexuality. Some factors to consider include: (a) parental attitudes toward sexuality in general, (b) parental attitudes toward homosexuality, (c) parental attitudes toward other minority groups, and (d) the family's adherence to traditional religious beliefs.

Before proceeding, adolescents need to assess not only how sure they are of their parent or parents, but also whether or not they are prepared to deal with the consequences if they have predicted inaccurately.

2. **Examining motivation.** Although there are many good reasons for disclosure, it can be used as a way of hurting parents, precipitating a conflict, forcing rejection or testing. Gay or lesbian adolescents may have difficulty pinpointing and expressing their motives, but these must be explored to determine whether they are based on love or anger, self-preservation or self-destruction.

Planning the Disclosure

1. **The Message.** Youngsters must be clear about what they mean to convey to their parents when they come out. Usually the message for parents is more than simply, "I'm a lesbian," or "I'm gay." It may be "I'm gay and I feel OK about that," or "I think I'm gay," or "I'm gay and I'm having trouble coming to terms with that," or "I'm in love with someone of the same sex." The message must state clearly what is expected from parents — support? acknowledgement? Rehearsing the message can enable youngsters to state it clearly and calmly. It may have to be repeated more than once, since the parents, in a highly emotional state, are unlikely to absorb all the information the first time.

In articulating the message, apologies such as "I'm sorry but I'm gay," should be avoided as should attributions of blame such as "It's your fault." It is also important to convey to the parents what it means to the child to be lesbian or gay, since the parents' concept of homosexuality and the child's will most likely be at odds. Above all, the good will behind the disclosure should be made explicit; the parents are being told out of love or a need to share (Weinberg, 1972).

Conveying all the necessary information can be facilitated if the adolescent is aware of the essentials of effective communication such as speaking clearly, making eye contact, avoiding jargon that parents may not understand, and checking periodically to make sure the message is being heard accurately.

2. **Method.** There are several ways to make a disclosure to parents. Even young people who decide to use a letter initially must prepare for an eventual face-to-face meeting with their parents.

Adolescents should begin by indicating that they have something important to talk about and would like some uninterrupted time with their parents. Some may want to tell one parent first, often the mother. If this is the case they must be prepared for the "Don't tell your father/mother," response. It is unwise to make such promises under pressure (Weinberg, 1972).

The adolescent should assume responsibility for deciding beforehand the boundaries of the discussion. A barrage of questions like, "Won't you be lonely.... Won't people think you're sick.... Aren't you afraid of losing your job," and so on, can be thinly veiled attacks and need not be answered at this point. Individual youngsters will have different levels of comfort discussing intimate details with parents. They need not feel obligated to discuss things which, ordinarily, would be private. Youngsters should be prepared to end the discussion if it gets out of hand.

Youngsters may want an ally to be present for moral support — a worker, counsellor or friend for example. Whether alone or with support, adolescents should make the disclosure in a place from which they can exit easily if the discussion turns into a heated confrontation.

3. **Timing.** The timing of the disclosure is important for both the parents and children. Most adolescents are still dependent on their parents both financially and emotionally. Therefore, they must decide whether they can cope with an initial rejection or withdrawal, if it occurs, as well as with some long-term distancing. If adolescents are anticipating moving out of the house in the near future, going away to school or assuming a full-time job for example, they may want to consider putting off the disclosure until they are in a more independent position.

It is also important to question the timing from the parental point of view. If there are two parents, is that relationship shaky? Are there financial problems? Are one or both unemployed? Have there been any other crises in the family? If so, the parents may not be able to cope and the disclosure should be put off until it is more likely that the parents can deal with an event which for them is a crisis.

The disclosure itself should be made when there is ample time for discussion. Christmas, birthdays, the Stanley Cup playoffs or any other time when there are likely to be distractions are probably not the best times to expect full attention.

4. **Anticipating parents' reactions.** Parents will react to disclosure with a range of emotions and intensity. Sometimes the initial reaction is so negative that it seems that the parents will never accept their child, and yet, eventually they do. They may receive the information with equanimity,

offering support and concern. Some, already suspecting the truth (especially if the youth has left an intentional trail of hints and clues) or simply sensing that something is amiss, will feel some relief that the issue is out in the open.

Other parents may feel angry and bewildered, wondering why such a tragedy has befallen them. They may even try to deny the truth by suggesting that the homosexuality is "just a phase," or by urging the adolescent to seek psychiatric help in order to change.

Parents may feel guilty and wonder what they did to "make" their youngster homosexual. This guilt is exacerbated by unproved and antiquated theories which attribute homosexuality to upbringing. As one mother expressed, "I kept wondering what I had done wrong.... I kept going over his childhood in my head, trying to figure out what I had done wrong.... It's always the mother, isn't it?"

Parents might feel ashamed that they have a son or daughter who is "sick", and, not knowing any other parents of gay or lesbian children, will feel isolated in the belief that they are the only ones in the world.

Many parents go through a grieving process similar to losing a loved one. Indeed, in their eyes they have lost their child —at least they believe they have lost the hopes and aspirations for their child, as well as the possibility of grandchildren.

Parents worry about the well-being of their gay son or lesbian daughter. Above and beyond their concern about the child's mental health, they fear for their child's happiness and physical safety. Will s/he be beaten up for being gay? Will s/he lose his/her job and ruin his/her career? Parents worry about the promiscuity often associated with homosexuality, the possibility of AIDS or the loneliness of being without a nuclear family, and imagine their child growing older as an alienated, isolated outcast.

Sometimes youngsters have inaccurately predicted parents reaction, and are faced with extreme rejection. Some are expelled from the home. Sometimes they are "grounded," forbidden to see their gay or lesbian friends, and forced to participate in psychiatric treatment aimed at changing their sexual orientation. Because of the extreme range of possible reactions, adolescents must be prepared for any eventuality by planning ahead to provide support for themselves and their parents.

5. **Support for parents and children.** As a young gay male pointed out, "It took me four years to feel OK about being gay. I couldn't expect my parents to come to terms with it overnight."

As young gays and lesbians respond to their parents' upset, role reversal frequently takes place. They must demonstrate a degree of empathy and patience which is unusual for many adolescents. They become the educators, while their parents experience a process of coming to terms with homosexuality similar to their child's own struggle.

Following the disclosure — perhaps immediately, weeks or months afterward — the parents will want answers to questions and an opportunity to air both their concerns and their emotions. They need to hear that their gay or lesbian child is the same one they raised and nurtured through childhood and into adolescence. Their child's revelation does not suddenly make him/her a stranger. They also need to explore the meaning of being gay or lesbian. This will enable them to examine critically homosexual myths and stereotypes, and come to a realistic understanding of the implications for them and their child. Parents need to know that they are not alone, and that the sense of crisis, with its attendant onslaught of feelings, will eventually subside. Perhaps most important, they need to be made aware that the disclosure was an act of love, concern, and sharing.

During the parental movement toward acceptance, young people must be prepared to offer information, resources and people to contact, including if possible, other parents of lesbians and gay males. In some communities there may be a group called *Parents and Friends of Gays and Lesbians*. The bibliography at the end of this book includes some reading material for parents.

Lesbian and gay adolescents will also need support during the process. This support may be forthcoming from sympathetic siblings, aunts or uncles, friends, teachers, or counsellors. The role of a worker or a therapist can be particularly important during this time. Friends are essential allies. As one young man suggested, "Make sure you tell a friend before you tell your parents. Just in case they throw you out you'll have a place to stay."

Role of the Worker

The role of the worker or counsellor in the disclosure process is (a) to help the youngster decide whether or not to disclose, (b) to help the youngster plan the disclosure and prepare for the aftermath, (c) to act as a support for the adolescent in the aftermath, and (d) to respond to the parents' need for support by providing counselling or referring them to another professional.

After Disclosure

What does the future hold for the gay or lesbian youngster and the family? At best, it will take some time for the parents to come to terms with their homosexual child. Eventually, some come to perceive the disclosure as a gratifying and unifying gesture. Parents and youngsters can feel the closeness of having shared an important confidence. Parents may even be relieved to see that their child is happier for having come to terms with a homosexual orientation, and having unburdened him/herself of the secret. They may eventually perceive their youngster's sexual orientation to be as natural as the youngster does, and, when the time comes, will be able to find a place in the family for their son's or daughter's long-term partner.

Other parents will struggle, and may never fully accept their child, whose sexual orientation will become a subtle, ongoing source of tension. In a minority of families, the homosexuality of a youth will be the last straw in a poor parent-child relationship. The youngster may be rejected completely, and, have to prepare for no possible reconciliation. Ultimately, the outcome is dependant upon the individual's relationship to other members of the family and the strengths and weaknesses of the particular family.

Self-disclosure to parents is both an end and a beginning. No longer is the disclosure issue hanging over the youngster's head. Parents may now have answers to a number of puzzling questions. For better or worse, it can be the beginning of a new relationship between parent and youngster. New issues are presented. Which relatives should be told? Which family friends should be told? If the youngster is openly gay or lesbian, will the rest of the family feel repercussions in school, the workplace, or the community? For each family, the salience of these issues will vary, as will the family's desire to address them. The success of the process will depend upon the sensitivity of each family member to the needs of others.

CHAPTER 12

Lesbian or Gay Clients: Implications for Social Service Delivery

Service delivery to lesbian and gay adolescents raises a number of concerns for workers and administrators. In this chapter the following issues will be addressed: (a) generic versus special services; (b) issues for the heterosexual service provider; and (c) issues for the lesbian or gay service provider.

The Role of Generic and Special Services

The debate about the most effective context in which to provide services for lesbian and gay clients has, to date, focussed on the question of the relative benefits of special, as opposed to generic services. Those who favor special services make the following observations:

1. Many lesbian and gay adolescents will not use generic services because they perceive such services as anti-gay; whereas, they would use a special service openly identified as gay-affirmative.

2. A special service could have openly gay and lesbian staff who can empathize with the struggles of their clients and act as role models for their clients.

Proponents of generic services contend that:

1. Special services will ghettoize lesbian and gay clients.

2. Clients who are uncomfortable with their sexual orientation or who are fearful of being discovered will not use special services.

3. Generic social services will continue to have clients who are lesbian, gay, and sexually confused using their services for reasons other than sexual orientation. Therefore, workers in generic services need to develop the skills which are required to work effectively with these clients.

In fact, the answer lies in a combination of both types of services. Special services would provide counselling with a sensitivity to the issues important to lesbian and gay clients, in an atmosphere in which clients would feel safe. Ideally, the service could act as a funnel, routing lesbian and gay clients into generic community programs when required. For example, a youth needing job training could be placed in a generic job-training program, with the additional support of the gay-affirmative service for dealing with personal issues. At the same time, generic services need to be able to respond in a gay-affirmative way to homosexual clients. It is neither in the client's nor the agency's interest to avoid dealing with homosexual clients by referring them to special services.

Service provision for lesbian or gay clients in generic settings has implications for heterosexual workers, lesbian and gay workers, and for the agency itself. These implications will be discussed below.

Issues for the Heterosexual Worker

Few workers have had any opportunity in their formal training to learn about homosexuality or experience working with gay or lesbian clients. Heterosexual workers, especially if they have never met any gay men or lesbians, may believe that counselling a homosexual client is completely outside their realm of expertise. They may doubt that they possess the necessary skills to work with this client population and may wonder whether it is appropriate for a straight worker to counsel gay or lesbian clients.

Heterosexuality does not disqualify workers from being effective with homosexual clients. The counselling and interpersonal skills that are effective with straight clients will be effective in work with homosexual clients, *if coupled with* a gay-affirmative attitude. In fact, a gay-positive heterosexual can be valuable for the client who feels unaccepted. Given the prevailing attitudes about homosexuality with which most people were raised, an examination of attitudes and beliefs about homosexuality would be useful, as outlined in Chapter 5.

Issues for the Lesbian or Gay Worker

Gay or lesbian service providers have the potential to be valuable resources for co-workers and homosexual clients. They are likely to have a sensitivity to the issues, knowledge of community resources, and by their very presence they can be appropriate role models for clients who are lesbian and gay. It is unfortunate, therefore, that most lesbian or gay social service providers fear that their jobs would be in jeopardy if they were open about their sexuality in the workplace. Those who opt to be open have to deal with the response of fellow workers, supervisors, and possibly board members or funding agents. Beyond that they must decide if disclosure to any or all of their clients is appropriate. Further, they may be expected to act as resource persons for other workers. In the present context, disclosure to clients and their role as resource-persons are the pertinent issues.

Disclosure to clients
In the course of working with clients, workers might find it appropriate to reveal some personal things about themselves in response to clients' questions, or to share common experiences. In this context, workers might wonder whether or not to come out to clients. The answer depends upon the specific client-counsellor relationship. The first step in determining the answer is to isolate, momentarily, the issue of sexual orientation and ask whether self-disclosure of any personal issues is relevant or appropriate. For example, if the task at hand is to find the youngster employment or get into a school program, self-disclosure of any sort is not likely to be relevant. However, if the client-counsellor relationship is to be long-term, or, if it depends on establishing trust, then a degree of self-disclosure may be an integral part of the process. Here is the experience of one male worker with a gay client:

> I had been working with David for about five months, spending about six hours a week on life skills, when he told me that he thought he might be gay. We had a pretty good relationship by that point — I suppose that was why he felt he could tell me. He knew a few things about me, and had even been to my apartment one time when we cooked a meal together. At first I didn't know whether I should tell him that I was gay. But I did know that if I didn't tell him soon, I would lose the chance, and that if I told him later on, or if he found out accidentally from someone else, that it would look like I was trying to hide something — that I didn't trust him, or that *I* was ashamed of being gay. So I told him, and it worked out pretty well, because I think it was good for him to have that kind of role model.

Self-disclosure to a heterosexual client is also a sensitive issue. This is the experience of a female worker with a straight client:

> I had been contracted to work with Lisa for about five hours a week. Over a period of time we had talked about a lot of different things —

boys, sex, families.... She asked me if I had a boyfriend and I told her I didn't. Later she asked me if I wanted a boyfriend and if I ever wanted to get married. I realized that even though I could answer the question accurately without coming out to her, I knew that unless I told her I was a lesbian I wasn't being honest. It had taken so long to develop her trust, and here I was caught between sort of lying to her or telling her something that might really alienate her. I talked this over with my team, and finally decided to come out to Lisa. I think it threw her a bit. She seemed distant for a few weeks, but that settled down. I think to her I was Sarah the social worker, not Sarah the lesbian.

These examples illustrate instances in which self-disclosure worked out well. However, in other instances it may not be advisable — for example if the youth is extremely homophobic or if the parents would object strenuously to a gay or lesbian worker. The support and guidance of colleagues and supervisors is very valuable when weighing the potential consequences. Gays and lesbians who are not out in the workplace obviously cannot take advantage of this peer consultation, and may not feel they can risk disclosure to their client, since they are not "out" to their co-workers.

Lesbian and gay workers as resources
Professionals who are openly gay or lesbian can provide valuable information, act as role models for clients, and offer insights into clients' conflicts based on their own experiences. However, a homosexual is not necessarily an expert on homosexuality, any more than a heterosexual is, *ipso facto*, an expert on heterosexuality. Issues such as sex or ethnic or rural versus urban differences in the coming-out experience, may be beyond the expertise of individual gay and lesbian workers. Thus, if openly gay and lesbian professionals are to act as a resource, they need to become conversant with a variety of issues, and recognize their limitations.

Sometimes workers who are lesbian or gay are assumed to be the most suitable people to work with lesbian or gay clients. This is not necessarily so. Homosexual clients need not be matched with a homosexual worker any more than a Jewish client, for example, need be matched with a Jewish worker. Furthermore, some gay or lesbian clients, in particular those who are uncomfortable with their sexual orientation, may not even want a homosexual worker. When clients and workers are matched, a wide range of variables needs to be considered. Sexual orientation should not be permitted to obscure all the other things about clients and workers that make them unique as individuals and appropriate to work together.

Agency Policy
The provision of social services for gay and lesbian youth is a sensitive

issue. Certain vocal factions of the public believe that the only appropriate response to gay youth is to encourage them to change their sexual orientation. In the extreme instance, these factions perceive gay-affirmative services to be supporting a perverse, anti-social lifestyle. Hence, the issue has the potential to trigger a volatile public debate. To avoid contention, many mainstream social service agencies operate without clear policies and guidelines regarding youth who are gay or lesbian, or for that matter, personnel who are gay or lesbian, attempting, nevertheless, to provide gay-affirmative services.

In this vacuum, workers may feel restrained in their counselling practice by their perception of policy, whether accurate or not. They may doubt that support will be forthcoming for a gay-affirmative approach to counselling. They also may wonder if advocating safer sex, finding gay role models, utilizing the lesbian or gay community or requesting staff-training in this area will be perceived as "encouraging homosexuality." Yet, when the front-line workers and administration compare notes, they are frequently, but not always, in accord regarding provision of services for this client population. In either case, the lack of a policy or even a dialogue about a policy leaves workers in isolation, unclear as to whether they have the support they require to work effectively with gay and lesbian youth.

Gay and lesbian professionals feel particularly vulnerable in the absence of a clearly stated policy. They fear, often correctly, that coming out will jeopardize their careers. Gays and lesbians who work with children feel particularly vulnerable because of the erroneous characterization of homosexuals as child molesters. In the absence of a clear agency policy regarding gay and lesbian personnel, workers will hesitate to come out and supervisors will be unsure of how to respond to homosexual staff who are openly so. The resulting tension as the worker tries to keep the secret, may deprive the agency of a potentially valuable resource.

Conclusion

The ability of everyone involved to be open about attitudes and beliefs, about their own sexuality, and about specific policies regarding service provision to lesbian and gay clients will increase effectiveness, just as any improvement in communication improves client/worker and worker/agency relationships. The willingness of all professionals, not merely to tolerate or accept differences in clients and colleagues, but to cherish these differences eventually will lead to the realization that similarities and differences are merely two sides of the same coin.

Notes

1. The topic of AIDS will not be addressed in this book; however, for more information about AIDS, the following are recommended reading: Alyson, Sasha ed. (1988); *You Can Do Something About AIDS*, Stop AIDS Project, Boston. Bell, Ruth (1987); *Changing Bodies, Changing Lives*, Vintage Books, New York. Frumpkin, Lyn Roberts, and Leonard, John Martin (1987); *Questions and Answers on AIDS*, Medical Economics Books, Oradell, New Jersey. Kubler-Ross, Elizabeth (1987); *AIDS: The Ultimate Challenge*, MacMillan, New York. Preston, John and Swann, Glenn (1986); *Safe Sex: the ultimate erotic guide*, New American Library, New York and Scarborough, Ontario. Quackenbush, Marcia (1987), Educating Youth About AIDS; *Focus: A Review of AIDS Research*, Vol. 2, No. 3; AIDS Health Project, University of California, San Francisco. Schinazi, Raymond F. ed. (1988); *AIDS in Children, Adolescents, and Heterosexual Adults*, Elsevier, New York. Spurgeon, David (1988); *Understanding* AIDS: A Canadian Strategy, Key Porter Books, Toronto.

2. Until 1962 in the United States, sexual contact between persons of the same sex was a criminal offense in all the states. As of 1982 homosexual behavior was a criminal offense in 29 states, sometimes with penalties of up to 20 years in prison (Rivera, 1982).

3. Research such as the Blumstein and Schwartz (1983) study of couples shows that heterosexual and homosexual couples are comparable on a variety of dimensions of sexual activity including frequency of sexual activity. Studies of the sexual abuse of children indicate that homosexuals are no more likely than heterosexuals to molest children (Newton, 1978).

4. In more recent, but less publicized conceptualizations, Storms (1980) and Shively and DeCecco (1977) propose that sexual orientation is best depicted two-dimensionally, so that an individual could be rated separately on heterosexual attraction and homosexual attraction. According to this system, an individual could be high on one type of attraction and low on the other, high on both, or low on both. This eliminates the implication inherent in the Kinsey Scale that bisexuality is a "watered down mixture of the two extreme components, and that one form of sexual expression is at the expense of the other." (Gonsiorek, 1982, p. 59)

5. Until recently little attention was paid to people who described themselves as bisexual, that is, equally attracted sexually to both males and females. Some experts believed that there were no true bisexuals; they believed that everyone had a preference one way or the other. Bisexuals were not usually welcomed in lesbian or gay circles because gays and lesbians believed that bisexuals were really homosexuals who were too homophobic to admit it to themselves. It seems, however, that some people are indeed bisexual (see *Journal of Homosexuality*, Volumes 10 (3/4) and 11 (1/2)). When young clients describe themselves as bisexual, a number of possibilities exist: (a) They may be bisexual; (b) They may be going through a phase in the coming-out process and will drop the bisexual label when they feel more comfortable about identifying themselves as lesbian or gay; or (c) They may be calling themselves bisexual as the result of an isolated, experimental homosexual experience or because it is the fashion among their peers to label themselves that way. A worker may respond to ostensibly bisexual clients by exploring with them what it means to be bisexual and whether or not it poses problems for them.

6. A persistent myth about gay men is that they cross-dress, that is they enjoy wearing women's clothing. In fact, few gay men are cross-dressers and many cross-dressers are heterosexual men. In others words, homosexuality and cross-dressing are two separate phenomena.

Cross-dressing is a complex issue. Some heterosexual cross-dressers are sexually aroused by wearing women's clothing (Transvestic Fetishism). Other men cross-dress because psychologically they feel more comfortable in women's clothing but are not sexually aroused by the clothing (Gender Identity Disorder of Adolescence or Adulthood, Nontranssexual Type). Others do so for fun or entertainment as in the case of female impersonators. Some male prostitutes dress in female attire as part of their work, catering to male customers who seek sex with transvestites (another term for men who dress in women's clothing).

According to the *DSM-III-R*, true cross-dressers, that is, those who fall into one of the two diagnostic categories mentioned above, are rare. When young gay clients appear in make-up or in female clothing it is important to examine the underlying motivation. Adolescents may cross-dress for one of a number of reasons including (a) They are seeking attention; (b) They think that being gay means they are supposed to cross-dress; (c) They try to appear openly gay to avoid rejection later on, as if to say, "Reject me now before I get to know you." (d) They are trying out different roles in their attempt to discover for themselves the meaning of being gay. The worker will need to examine the client's motivation in order to put his cross-dressing into perspective.

7. Recently, there has been a reemergence of butch/femme role-playing within a small segment of the lesbian community. It is not, however, the same as the role-playing prior to the 1970s in that, presently, role-playing is not obligatory and seems to be more like play or dressing-up rather than a serious attempt to act like the extremes of either gender role.

8. For example, in the Bell et al. (1981) study of childhood experiences, 11% of heterosexual males and 28% of heterosexual females enjoyed gender-atypical activities as children. Fifty-four percent of gay males and 29% of lesbians reported not engaging in gender-atypical activities as children.

9. So-called effeminate behavior among some gay men has been likened to an accent. A gay man who becomes immersed in the gay community and culture may simply develop the style of speech and the mannerisms characteristic of that group of gays. A similar, perhaps more familiar process takes place when a person moves to New York and develops a New York accent and starts to talk with her/his hands. It has also been observed that effeminacy is more common among males from backgrounds which expose them to rigid gender roles, for example, males from Hispanic or working-class backgrounds (Joyce Hunter, personal communication, 1986). This is another example of cultural influences on cross-gender behavior.

10. The usual conclusion about the connection between gender role and homo- sexuality is that atypical gender role and homosexuality are biologically based and biologically linked. However, Joseph Harry (1982) proposes an alternate hypothesis. He suggests that "once the individual has departed from conven- tional ... gender-appropriate behavior he then is freed to drift from one form of erotic behaviour to another without constraint." (p. 6) Presumably, this could work the other way around as well. Individuals who perceive themselves to be deviant because of their erotic attraction to the same sex may be freed to engage in gender-atypical behaviors.

11. "The Boys in the Band" (released in 1970, directed by William Friedkin) and "La Cages aux Folles" (released in 1979, directed by Edouard Molinaro) are movies in which the major characters are stereotypical gay men. The former portrays a particularly destructive gay lifestyle, while the latter humorously portrays a drag queen. *The Children's Hour*, written by Lillian Hellman (1942), is a story, based on an actual event, about two female school teachers who are accused by a student of being lesbians. One of them hangs herself in the end. *The Well of Loneliness* written by Radclyffe Hall in 1928 is the tragic story of a very masculine lesbian who ultimately loses her petite, feminine lover to a man. The book has become a cult classic and the phrase, "the love that dares not speak its name," which has become a watchword in lesbian and gay culture, is a quotation from this book.

12. It is important to note that there are some fundamental differences between the intimate relationships of lesbians and those of gay men. Although both types of relationships share the commonality of being homosexual, the dynamics between two male partners and two female partners are different. See Moses and Hawkins (1982) and Blumstein and Schwartz (1983) for a comprehensive discussion of homosexual relationships. For discussions of issues for lesbian couples in particular, see Burch (1987), Kaufman, et al. (1984) and Krestan and Bebko (1980).

13. The term "promiscuity" has a negative and judgemental tone. The word is used here for lack of a better one and is not meant to be pejorative. It simply indicates having a variety of sexual partners. It is recognised that definitions of what constitutes promiscuity is variable and subjective.

14. The topic of lesbian and gay parenting will not be explored in this book. However, it is important to note that the possibility of raising children is becoming a viable choice for gay men, and especially for lesbians. Being raised by gay or lesbian parents appears to have no detrimental effects on children and they seem to be no more likely than children raised by heterosexual parents to grow up to be homosexual (Gantz, 1983; Golombek, Spenser, & Rutter, 1983; Green, 1978; Green, et al., 1986; Hoeffer, 1981; Kirkpatrick & Smith, 1981; Lewis, 1980; Miller, Jacobsen, & Bigner, 1981).

15. However, Ontario, Quebec and Manitoba have included clauses in their Human Rights Codes prohibiting discrimination on the basis of sexual orientation.

16. The victim, Ronald Pettine, a political aide to Congressman Morris Udall, was murdered in 1977. The last of his three killers was sentenced in May, 1979. The major issue is not the violence, but the casual acceptance by the patrons of the bar of both the violence and the bragging about the violence.

17. Allport's book offers a good summary of this research.

18. An inaccurate term since so called effeminate behavior has little to do with the way women move, walk or talk. It is a form of male behavior that differs from the established cultural norm. Similarly, "butch" behavior by the lesbian is not masculine behavior.

References

Albro, J.C., & Tully, C. (1979). A study of lesbian lifestyles in the homosexual micro-culture and the heterosexual macro-culture. *Journal of Homosexuality, 4* (4), 331-344.

Allport, G. (1958). *The nature of prejudice.* Garden City, N.Y., Doubleday.

American Psychiatric Association (1983). *Diagnostic and statistical manual of mental disorders (3rd ed.) (DSM-III).* Washington, DC: American Psychiatric Association.

American Psychiatric Association (1987). *Diagnostic and statistical manual of mental disorders (3rd ed.): Revised (DSM-III-R).* Washington, DC: American Psychiatric Association.

Bayer, R. (1981). *Homosexuality and American psychiatry.* New York: Basic.

Bayley, B.H. (1974). The policeman and the homosexual. *New Sociology, 1,* 18-52.

Belitsos, G. (1983). Rural gay and lesbian youth: Implications for the youth worker. In S. Bergstrom, & L. Cruz (Eds.), *Counselling lesbian and gay male youth.* Washington: National Network of Runaway and Youth Service.

Bell, A.P., & Weinberg, M.S. (1978). *Homosexualities: A study of diversity among men and women.* New York: Simon and Schuster.

Bell, A.P., Weinberg, M., & Hammersmith, S. (1981). *Sexual preference: Its development in men and women.* Bloomington: Indiana University Press.

Berger, G., Hank, L., Rauzi, T., & Simkins, L. (1987). Detection of sexual orientation by heterosexuals and homosexuals. *Journal of Homosexuality, 13,* 83-100.

Bergler, E. (1957). *Homosexuality: Disease or way of life.* New York: Hill and Wang.

Bieber, I., Dain, H., Dince, P., Drellich, M., Grand, H., Gundlach, R., Dremer, M., Rifkin, A., Wilbur, C., & Bieber, T. (1962). *Homosexuality: A psychoanalytic study.* New York: Basic.

Blumstein, P., & Schwartz, P. (1983). *American Couples.* New York: William Morrow.

Brooks, V. (1981). *Minority stress and lesbian women.* Toronto: Lexington.

Bullough, V.L. (1981). *Homosexuality: A history.* New York: American Library Publishing.

Burch, B. (1987). Barriers to intimacy: Conflicts over power, dependency, and nurturing in lesbian relationships. In Boston Lesbian Psychologies Collective (Eds.), *Lesbian psychologies: Exploration and challenges.* Chicago: University of Illinois Press.

Cardell, M., Finn, S., & Marecek, J. (1981). Sex-role identity, sex-role behavior, and satisfaction in heterosexual, lesbian, and gay male couples. *Psychology of Women Quarterly, 5,* 488-491.

Cass, V.C. (1979). Homosexual identity formation: A theoretical model. *Journal of Homosexuality, 4* (3), 219-235.

Coleman, E. (1982). Developmental stages in the coming-out process. *Journal of Homosexuality, 7* (2/3), 31-43.

Comfort, A. (1987). *The joy of sex.* New York: Simon & Schuster.

Corbett, S.L., Troiden, R.R., & Dodder, R.A. (1977). Tolerance as a correlate of experience with stigma: The case of the homosexual. *Journal of Homosexuality, 3* (1), 3-14.

Cotton, W.L. (1975). Social and sexual relationships of lesbians. *Journal of Sex Research, 11*, 138-148.

Cronin, D.M. (1974). Coming out among lesbians. In E. Goode, & R.R. Troiden (Eds.), *Sexual deviance and sexual deviants*. New York: Morrow.

Dailey, D.M. (1977). Legitimacy and permanence in the gay relationship: Some intervention alternatives. *Journal of Social Welfare, 4*, 81-88.

Dailey, D.M. (1979). Adjustment of heterosexual and homosexual couples in pairing relationships. *Journal of Sex Research, 15*, 143-157.

Dank, B. (1971). Coming out in the gay world. *Psychiatry, 34*, 180-197.

Davison, G. (1977). Homosexuality: The ethical challenge. *Journal of Homosexuality, 2* (3), 195-204.

Davison, G.C., & Wilson, G.T. (1973). Attitudes of behavior therapists toward homosexuality. *Behavior Therapy, 4*, 686-696.

De Monteflores, C., & Schultz, S. (1978). Coming out: Similarities and differences for lesbians and gay men. *Journal of Social Issues, 34*, 59-72.

Douce, L. (1985). *Counselling gay and lesbian clients: A university internship training model*. Paper presented at the Annual Meeting of the American Psychological Association, Los Angeles.

Eisner, M. (1982). *An investigation of the coming-out process, lifestyle, and sex-role orientation of lesbians*. Unpublished doctoral dissertation, York University, North York, Ontario.

Epstein, J. (1970). Homo/Hetero: The struggle for sexual identity. *Harper's, 241*, 36-51.

Erikson, E.H. (1963). *Childhood and society*. New York: Norton.

Freud, S. (1905). Three essays on the theory of sexuality. In J. Strachy (Ed), *The standard edition of the complete psychological works of Sigmund Freud*, Vol 7. London: Hogarth (1974).

Gagnon, J.H., & Simon, W. (1973). A conformity greater than deviance: The lesbian. In J.H. Gagnon, & W. Simon (Eds.), *Sexual conduct: The social sources of human sexuality*. Chicago: Aldine.

Gantz, J. (1983). *Whose child cries: Children of gay parents talk about their lives*. Rolling Hills Estate, CA: Jalmar.

Glausen, B. (Director & Producer) (1980). *Michael, a gay son* [Film]. Toronto: Canadian Filmmakers Distribution Centre.

Goffman, E. (1963). *Stigma: Notes on the management of spoiled identity*. Englewood Cliffs, NJ: Prentice Hall.

Golden, C. (1987). Diversity and variability in women's sexual identities. In Boston Lesbian Psychologies Collective (Eds.), *Lesbian psychologies: Explorations and challenges*. Chicago: University of Illinois Press.

Golombek, S., Spenser, A., & Rutter, M. (1983). Children in lesbian and single-parent households: Psychosexual and psychiatric appraisal. *Journal of Child Psychology and Psychiatry, 24,* 551-572.

Gonsiorek, J.C. (1982). Introduction. In W. Paul et al (Eds.), *Homosexuality: Social, psychological, and biological issues*. Beverly Hills: Sage.

Gonsiorek, J.C. (1982a). Results of psychological testing on homosexual populations. In W. Paul et al (Eds.), *Homosexuality: Social, psychological, and biological issues*. Beverly Hills: Sage.

Green, R. (1978). Sexual identity of 37 children raised by homosexual or transsexual parents. *American Journal of Psychiatry, 135,* 692-697.

Green, R. (1980). Patterns of sexual identity in childhood. In J. Marmor (Ed.), *Homosexual behavior: A modern reappraisal*. New York: Basic.

Green, R., Mandel, J., Hotvedt, M., Gray, J., & Smith, L. (1986). Lesbian mothers and their children: A comparison with solo parent heterosexual mothers and their children. *Archives of Sexual Behavior, 15* (2), 167-184.

Grier, W., & Cobbs, P. (1968). *Black rage*. New York: Basic.

Hall, R. (1976). *The well of loneliness*. London: Barrie & Jenkins. (Original work published 1928)

Harry, J. (1982). *Gay children grow up*. New York: Praeger.

Harry, J. (1983). Defeminization and adult psychological well-being among male homosexuals. *Archives of Sexual Behavior, 12* (1), 1-19.

Hellman, L. (1942). *Four plays*. New York: Modern Library.

Henley, N.M., & Pincus, F. (1978). Interrelationship of sexist, racist, and antihomosexual attitudes. *Psychological Reports, 42,* 83-90.

Hedblom, J.H., & Hartman, J.J. (1980). Research on lesbianism: Selected effects of time, geographic location, and data collection techniques. *Archives of Sexual Behavior, 9,* 217-234.

Heron, A. (1983). *One teenager in ten.* Boston: Alyson.

Hetrick, E., & Martin, D. (1983). Ego-dystonic homosexuality: A developmental view. In E. Hetrick, & T. Stein (Eds.), *Psychotherapy with homosexuals.* Washington, DC: American Psychiatric Press.

Hoeffer, B. (1981). Children's acquisition of sex-role behavior in lesbian-mother families. *American Journal of Orthopsychiatry, 51,* 536-544.

Humphries, L. (1970). *Tearoom trade: Impersonal sex in public places.* Chicago: Aldine.

Hunt, M. (1974). *Sexual behavior in the 1970s.* Chicago: Playboy Press.

Josselson, R. (1980). Ego development in adolescence. In J. Adelson (Ed.), *Handbook of adolescent psychology.* Toronto: Wiley.

Karr, R.G. (1981). Homosexual labeling and the male role. In J.W. Chesebro (Ed.), *Gayspeak — Gay male and lesbian communication.* New York: Pilgrim.

Katz, J.N. (1983). *Gay/lesbian almanac: A new documentary.* New York: Harper & Row.

Kaufman, P., Harrison, E., & Hyde, M.L. (1984). Distancing for intimacy in lesbian relationships. *American Journal of Psychiatry, 141* (4), 530-533.

Kaye, H., Bert, S., Clare, J., Eleston, M., Gershwin, B., Gershwin, P., Kagan, L., Torda, C., & Wilbur, C. (1967). Homosexuality in women. *Archives of General Psychiatry, 17,* 626-634.

Kinsey, A.C., Pomeroy, W.B., & Martin, C.E. (1948). *Sexual behavior in the human male.* Philadelphia: W.B. Saunders.

Kinsey, A.C., Pomeroy, W.B., Martin, C.E., & Gebhard, P.H. (1953). *Sexual behavior in the human female.* Philadelphia: W.B. Saunders.

Kirkpatrick, M., Smith, C., & Roy, R. (1981). Lesbian mothers and their children: A comparative study. *American Journal of Orthopsychiatry, 51,* 545-551.

Kourney, R.F. (1987). Suicide among homosexual adolescents. *Journal of Homosexuality, 13,* 111-117.

Krestan, J., & Bebko, C. (1980). The problem of fusion in the lesbian relationship. *Family Process, 19,* September, 277-289.

Krulewitz, J.E., & Nash, J.E. (1980). Effects of sex-role attitudes and similarity on men's rejection of male homosexuals. *Journal of Personality and Social Psychology, 38,* 67-74.

Kurdek, L.A., & Schmitt, J.P. (1987). Perceived emotional support from family and friends in members of homosexual, married and heterosexual cohabiting couples. *Journal of Homosexuality, 14* (3/4), 57-68.

Laing, R.D. (1965). *The divided self.* Baltimore: Pelican.

Laner, M.R., & Laner, R.H. (1980). Sexual preference or personal style? Why lesbians are disliked. *Journal of Homosexuality, 4* (4), 339-405.

Langevin, R. (1984). *Can homosexuality be changed?* Paper presented at the Annual Meeting of the Ontario Psychological Association, Ottawa.

Lee, J.A. (1977). Going public: A study in the sociology of homosexual liberation. *Journal of Homosexuality, 3,* 49-78.

Lewis, K.G. (1980). Children of lesbians: Their point of view. *Social Work,* May, 198-203.

Lynch, L. (1985). *Swashbuckler.* Tallahassee FL: Naiad Press.

Lynch, J., & Reilly, M.E. (1985). *Journal of Homosexuality, 12* (2), 53-59.

MacDonald, A.P., & Games, R.G. (1974). Some characteristics of those who hold positive and negative attitudes towards homosexuals. *Journal of Homosexuality, 1,* 9-27.

Malyon, A.K. (1982). Biphasic aspects of homosexual identity formation. *Psychotherapy: Theory, research and practice, 19* (3), 335-340.

Marmor, J. (1980). Overview: The multiple roots of homosexual behavior. In J. Marmor (Ed.), *Homosexual behavior: A modern reappraisal.* New York: Basic.

Martin, A.D., (1982). Learning to hide: The socialization of the gay adolescent. In S.C. Feinstein, J.G. Looney, A. Schwartzberg, & A. Scrosky (Eds.), *Adolescent psychiatry: Developmental and clinical studies, Vol. 10.* Chicago: University of Chicago Press.

Martin, A.D. (1984). The perennial Canaanites: The sin of homosexuality. *Etc.: A Review of General Semantics, 41,* 340—361.

Martin, A.D. (1984a). The emperor's new clothes: Modern attempts to change sexual orientation. In E. Hetrick, & T. Stein (Eds.), *Innovations in psychotherapy with homosexuals.* Washington: American Psychiatric Association.

Miller, J., Jacobsen, R., & Bigner, J. (1981). The child's home environment for lesbian versus heterosexual mothers: A neglected area of research. *Journal of Homosexuality, 7* (1), 49-56.

McDonald, A.P., & Games, R.G. (1974). Some characteristics of those who hold positive and negative attitudes towards homosexuals. *Journal of Homosexuality, 1,* 5-8.

McDonald, G. (1982). Individual differences in the coming-out process for gay men: Implications for theoretical models. *Journal of Homosexuality, 8,* 47-60.

Minnigerode, F.A. (1976). Age-status labeling in homosexual men. *Journal of Homosexuality, 1* (3), 273-276.

Money, J. (1980). Genetic and chromosomal aspects of homosexual etiology. In J. Marmor (Ed.), *Homosexual behavior: A modern reappraisal.* New York: Basic.

Morin, S., Taylor, K., & Kielman, S. (1975). *Gay is beautiful at a distance.* Paper presented at the Annual Meeting of the American Psychological Association.

Moses, A.E., & Bruckner, J.A. (1982). The special problems of rural gay clients. In A.E. Moses, & R.O. Hawkins (Eds.), *Counseling lesbian women and gay men: A life-issues approach.* Toronto: Mosby.

Moses, A.E., & Hawkins, R.O. (1982). Lesbians' and gay men's relationships. In A.E. Moses, & R.O. Hawkins (Eds.), *Counseling lesbian women and gay men: A life-issues approach.* Toronto: Mosby.

Nelson, J. (1978). *Embodiment.* Minneapolis: Augsburg.

Newton, D.E. (1978). Homosexual behavior and child molestation: A review of the evidence. *Adolescence, 13* (49).

Patterson, I. (1985). Confessions of a high school faggot. *The Body Politic,* May.

Paul, W., & Weinrich, J.D. (1982). Whom and what we study: Definition and scope of sexual orientation. In W. Paul et al. (Eds.), *Homosexuality: Social, psychological, and biological issues.* Beverly Hills: Sage.

Peters, H. (1982). The legal rights of gays. In A.E. Moses, & R.O. Hawkins (Eds.), *Counselling lesbian women and gay men: A life-issues approach.* Toronto: Mosby.

Rivera, R. (1982). Homosexuality and the law. In W. Paul et al. (Eds.), *Homosexuality: Social, psychological, and biological issues.* Beverly Hills: Sage.

Rofes, E.E. (1983). *Lesbians, gay men and suicide.* San Francisco: Grey Fox.

Ross, M.W. (1983). Femininity, masculinity and sexual orientation: Some cross-cultural comparisons. *Journal of Homosexuality, 9* (1), 27-36.

Saghir, M.T., & Robbins, E. (1973). *Male and female homosexuality: A comprehensive investigation.* Baltimore: Williams & Wilkins.

San Miguel, C.L., & Millham, J. (1976). The role of cognitive & situational variables in aggression toward homosexuals. *Journal of Homosexuality, 2* (1), 11-27.

Sanders, R., Bain, J., & Langevin, R. (1985). Peripheral sex hormones, homosexuality, and gender identity. In R. Langevin (Ed.), *Erotic preference, gender identity, and aggression in men.* Hillsdale, NJ: Laurence Erlbaum.

Schneider, M. (1985). *Developmental milestones in the lives of lesbian and gay adolescents.* Paper presented at the Annual Meeting of the American Orthopsychiatric Association, New York.

Schneider, M. (1986). The relationships of cohabiting lesbian and heterosexual couples: A comparison. *Psychology of Women Quarterly, 10,* 234-239.

Schneider, M. (in press). Sappho was a right-on adolescent: Growing up lesbian. *Journal of Homosexuality.*

Schneider, M., & Tremble, B. (1985). *Enhancing social service delivery to gay and lesbian adolescents.* Paper presented at the Annual Meeting of the American Orthopsychiatric Association, New York.

Schneider, M., & Tremble, B. (1985a). *The gay hustler: The relevance of sexual orientation.* Paper presented at the Annual Meeting of the Northeastern Region of the Child Welfare League of America, Portland, Maine.

Shively, M.G., & Dececco, J.P. (1977). Components of sexual identity. *Journal of Homosexuality, 3,* 41-48.

Silverstein, C., & White, E. (1977). *The joy of gay sex.* New York: Crown.

Smith, K.T. (1971). Homophobia: A tentative personality profile. *Psychological Reports, 29,* 1091-1094.

Smith, M.F., & Dilenno, J. (1979). *Sexual inversion: The questions: the church's answer.* Boston: Daughters of St. Paul.

Steffenmeir, D., & Steffenmeir, R. (1978). Sexual differences in reactions to homosexuals: Research continuities and further developments. *Journal of Sex Roles, 10,* 52-58.

Storms, M.D. (1978). Sexual orientation and self-perception. In P. Pliner et al. (Eds.), *Advances in the study of communication and affect: Vol. 5. Perception of emotion in self and others.* New York: Plenum.

Storms, M.D. (1980). Theories of sexual orientation. *Journal of Personality and Social Psychology, 38,* 783-792.

Tanner, D. (1978). *The lesbian couple.* Lexington: Lexington Books.

Tavris, C., & Offir, C. (1977). *The longest war: Sex differences in perspective.* New York: Harcourt Brace Jovanovich.

Tourney, G. (1980). Hormones and homosexuality. In J. Marmor (Ed.), *Homosexual behavior: a modern reappraisal.* New York: Basic.

Tremble, B. (director), & Central Toronto Youth Services (producer) (1985). *My family/Myself* [video]. Toronto: Central Toronto Youth Services.

Troiden, R.R. (1979). Becoming homosexual: A model of gay identity acquisition. *Psychiatry, 42* (4), 362-373.

Tuller, N.R. (1978). Couples: The hidden segment of the gay world. *Journal of Homosexuality, 3* (4), 331-343.

Voth, H. (1977). *The castrated family.* Kansas City, MO: Sheed, Andrews, & McMeel.

Warren, C.A. (1974). *Identity and community in the gay world.* New York: Wiley.

Weinberg, G. (1972). *Society and the healthy homosexual.* Garden City, NJ: Anchor Press/Doubleday.

Weinberg, M.S., & Williams, C.F. (1974). *Male Homosexuals.* New York: Oxford University Press.

Whitam, F. (1977). Childhood indicators of male homosexuality. *Archives of Sexual Behavior, 6,* 89-96.

Woolf, H.B. (Ed.) (1982). *Webster's New College Dictionary.* Toronto: Thomas Allen.

Extended Reading List

General Information

Bell, A.P., Weinberg, M.S., & Hammersmith, S.K. (1981). *Sexual preference: Its development in men and women.* Bloomington: Indiana University Press.

Hetrick, E., & Stein, T. (1984). *Innovations in psychotherapy with homosexuals.* Washington: American Psychiatric Association.

Journal of Homosexuality: A multi-disciplinary journal publishing research and theoretical papers on homosexuality. Special editions include bisexuality, homophobia, sex roles. An issue is planned to discuss gay and lesbian adolescents.

Malyon, A. (1982). Biphasic aspects of homosexual identity formation. *Psychotherapy, theory, research and practice, 19,* 335-340.

Malyon, A. (1980). The homosexual adolescent: Developmental issues and social bias. *Child Welfare, 60,* 321-330.

Marmor, J. (Ed.) (1980). *Homosexual behavior: A modern reappraisal.* New York: Basic. Discussions of causal theory, history, cross cultural differences, clinical issues, and cultural, legal, and religious issues.

Moses, A., & Hawkins, R. (1982). *Counselling lesbian women and gay men.* Toronto: Mosby. Discussions of attitudes, coming out, aging, gay and lesbian parenting, relationships, lifestyle issues, third world lesbians and gays.

The Coming Out Process

Cass, V. (1979). Homosexual identity formation: A theoretical model. *Journal of Homosexuality, 4,* 219-235.

Coleman, E. (1982). Developmental stages of the coming out process. *American Behavioural Scientist, 25,* 31-43.

Troiden, R. (1979). Becoming homosexual: A model of gay identity acquisition. *Psychiatry, 42,* 362-373.

Weinberg, T. (1978). On "doing" and "being" gay: Sexual behaviour and homosexual male self-identity. *Journal of Homosexuality, 4,* 143-156.

Stanley J., & Wolfe, S. (1980). *The coming out stories.* Watertown, Mass.: Persephone Press.

Books for Parents and Youngsters

Borhek, M. (1983). *Coming out to parents.* New York: Pilgrim.

Fairchild, B., & Haywood, N. (1979). *Now that you know: What every parent should know about homosexuality.* New York: Harcourt, Brace, Jovanovich.

Griffin, C.W., Wirth, M.J., & Wirth, A.G. (1986). *Beyond acceptance: Parents of lesbians and gays talk about their experiences.* Englewood Cliffs, NJ: Prentice-Hall.

Hanckel, F., & Cunningham, J. (1979). *A way of life, a way of love: A young person's introduction to what it means to be gay.* New York: Lothrop, Lee, & Shepard.

Myers, M.F. (1982). Counselling the parents of young homosexual male patients. In J.C. Gonsiorek (Ed.), *Homosexuality and psychotherapy.* New York: Haworth.

Silverstein, C. (1979). *A family matter.* New York: McGraw Hill.

The Lesbian Experience

Boston Lesbian Psychologies Collective (1987). *Lesbian psychologies: Explorations and challenges.* Chicago: University of Illinois Press.

Darty, T., & Potter, S. (1984). *Women-identified women.* Palo Alto: Mayfield. Discussion of coming out, relationships, older lesbians, third world lesbians, law, motherhood, health care, culture and community. Includes a foundational article by Adrienne Rich titled "Compulsory Heterosexuality and Lesbian Existence."

Faderman, L. (1981). *Surpassing the love of men: Romantic friendship and love between women from the Renaissance to the present.* New York: Morrow.

Relationships

Blumstein, P., & Schwartz, P. (1983). *American couples.* New York: Morrow.

Mendola, M. (1980). *The Mendola Report: A new look at gay couples* New York: Crown.

From a Religious Perspective

Beck E. (1982). *Nice Jewish girls: A lesbian anthology.* Trumansburg, N.Y.: Crossing Press.

Nelson, J. (1978). *Embodiment: An approach to sexuality and Christian theology.* Minneapolis: Augsburg.

Glossary

Bisexual: A person who is equally attracted to persons of the same and opposite sex.

Coming Out, or the Coming-Out Process:

1) "The developmental process through which gay and lesbian people recognize their sexual preferences and integrate this knowledge into their personal and social lives" (DeMonteflores & Schultz, 1978, p. 59).

2) Can also be used to mean "disclosure," as in "I just came out to my parents."

Cross-Dresser: (see Transvestite)

Gay: Homosexual. Can refer to both males and females, but increasingly is being used only to refer to men.

Gender Role: The characteristics of an individual which are culturally defined as masculine or feminine.

Heterosexual Assumption: The assumption that everyone is heterosexual unless otherwise indicated.

Homophobia: Dislike or fear of homosexuals as a group.

Homosexual: A male or female person whose sexual attraction, both physical and affectational, is for people of the same sex. Because the term is associated historically with the medical model of homosexuality, most homosexuals prefer the terms lesbian or gay.

Kinsey Scale: A seven-point continuum developed by Alfred Kinsey and his associates to describe sexual orientation. The scale ranges from exclusive heterosexuality to exclusive homosexuality, with all possible gradations in between. Most people are located somewhere between the two extremes.

Lesbian: A female homosexual.

Sex: The biological status as a female or male.

Sexual Identity: An individual's sense of self as male or female.

Sexual Orientation or Sexual Preference: The attraction of an individual to persons of the same or opposite sex, or both. Three sexual orientations are labeled: heterosexual, homosexual, and bisexual. (see Kinsey Scale)

Transsexual: A person whose sexual identity is different from her or his sex. For example, a biological male who would describe himself as a woman trapped inside a man's body. Transsexuals often request sex-change operations.

Transvestite: A man who enjoys dressing in women's clothing.

Index

TOM W. SMITH "ADULT
SEXUAL BEHAVIOR IN 1989,
NUMBER OF PARTNERS, FREQUENCY,
RISK." P.O.R.C., UNIV.
OF CHICAGO, NOV. 1989
GSS TOPICAL REPORT #18

(REPORTS ON BASIS OF
RANDOM SAMPLING THAT
1-3% OF POPULATION
IS HOMOSEXUAL)

WARNER MEMORIAL LIBRARY
EASTERN UNIVERSITY
ST. DAVIDS, PA 19087-3696